JOURNALING
The Ultimate Self-Improvement

An Essential and Definitive Guide on How to Write a Journal and Unlock Your True Power

Michael Stack

© **Copyright 2021 - All rights reserved.**

The content contained within this book may not be reproduced, duplicated or transmitted without direct written permission from the author or the publisher.

Under no circumstances will any blame or legal responsibility be held against the publisher, or author, for any damages, reparation, or monetary loss due to the information contained within this book, either directly or indirectly.

Legal Notice:

This book is copyright protected. It is only for personal use. You cannot amend, distribute, sell, use, quote or paraphrase any part, or the content within this book, without the consent of the author or publisher.

Disclaimer Notice:

Please note the information contained within this document is for educational and entertainment purposes only. All effort has been executed to present accurate, up to date, reliable, complete information. No warranties of any kind are declared or implied. Readers acknowledge that the author is not engaged in the rendering of legal, financial, medical or professional advice. The content within this book has been derived from various sources. Please consult a licensed professional before attempting any techniques outlined in this book.

By reading this document, the reader agrees that under no circumstances is the author responsible for any losses, direct or indirect, that are incurred as a result of the use of the information contained within this document, including, but not limited to, errors, omissions, or inaccuracies.

TABLE OF CONTENTS

INTRODUCTION..1

CHAPTER 1 9

  THE LOW-DOWN

    The Definition of a Journal

    Journaling Up Until Today

      The Timeline of the Journal

      Historical Journal Writers

    The Benefits of Journaling

      Successful Journal Writers

      Testimonies

      What Does This Mean for You?

CHAPTER 2 24

  HOW TO JOURNAL TODAY

    Choosing When to journal

    Making Space for Journaling

      Finding Time in a Busy World

      Creating Solitude for Yourself

Turning Journaling Into a Habit

Writing Your Journal

Journal prompts

My Tips

CHAPTER 3 .... **48**

THE VALUE OF JOURNALING

Mental Benefits

Metacognition and Thought Access

Awareness

Stress Management

Creating Positive Emotions

Reducing Negative Emotions

Time and Energy

Achieving Goals

Physical Benefits

Effects of Reducing Stress and Improving Mood

Immune System Improvement

CHAPTER 4 .... **72**

TRICKS OF THE TRADE

Bullet Journaling

Character Sketches

Clustering/Mind Mapping

Captured Moments

Time Capsule

Unsent Letters

Dialogues

Lists

Worst Case Scenario

Goal Setting

Stream of Consciousness

Dream Journaling

Non-Dominant Hand

CHAPTER 5 99

PERSONAL DEVELOPMENT

Relationship With Therapy

Similarities Between Journaling and Therapy

How Journaling can Complement Therapy

Journaling With a Purpose

Managing Emotions

Increasing Self-Esteem and Self-Love

Increasing Confidence

Affirmations

Coping With Trauma

Stress Management

Improving Organization

Increasing Happiness

Soothing Anxiety

Mindfulness

Manifestations
CONCLUSION 124
REFERENCES 128

Your Free Gift

As a way of saying thanks for your purchase, I'm giving you a free digital copy of *Top 10 Ways to Achieve All Your Goals* that's exclusive to readers of this book.

This shortlist, paired with this book, will provide you with a rigid foundation to tackle whatever obstacles are looming in your life. Enter the URL below to gain free instant access.

https://michaelstackauthor.gr8.com/

INTRODUCTION

Do you feel as if you are stuck in place while the world moves around you? This might be professionally, creatively, or in your personal life. You might not have a clear vision of what you want your life to be like, and feel as if you're just reacting to the actions of others, leaving you craving more. Or perhaps you do have clear aims and aspirations, a vision of your ideal life, that you haven't been able to put into practice, whether due to external factors stopping you, or issues within you preventing you. While others achieve their goals, you might feel as though you are being left behind, while they leap forward onto new achievements and activities. The advice they give you doesn't seem to work for you, leaving you frustrated.

If you are reading this book, you might identify with these feelings of frustration, sensing the same lack of momentum in your own life. It can be easy when you face these struggles to feel as though you are just incapable of achieving your goals, or that your ideal life is a dream you will never get to actually live. This can become a cycle of defeat; a self-fulfilling prophecy that prevents you from seeing your life clearly without the fog of frustration that clouds you.

I want to make it clear now that these negative thoughts are untrue, and that the fog of frustration is just that, and can easily be blown away. You have taken the first step towards blowing away these thoughts, and the first step towards achieving your dream life, by picking up this book. With the tips and skills you learn in these pages, you will be firmly in the driving seat of your own life, no longer a passenger on an unknown journey, but a confident driver able to navigate roadblocks with ease, and steer yourself onto a new highway of potential.

The first step on this journey is to remove any feelings of fear, embarrassment or inferiority you might have acquired through previous setbacks. These feelings may feel like they protect you, preventing you from experiencing more embarrassment or failure, but they do so by presenting you with a false version of yourself that limits your potential failures and your potential success.

Using this guide, you will learn to express yourself without fear, starting in the safe space of your journal, and start to see a true picture of yourself, and how you live your life. Journaling about your life will also help you gain some distance and perspective, and you will be able to examine past situations clearly, assessing what worked for you and what other options you could have taken. You will then be able to apply this clarity to the future, analysing potential roadblocks and formulating solutions that will allow you to speed past them, and into the next stage of your new reality.

Having personally experienced the value of journaling, I wanted to put together my experience and knowledge to share with the world, sharing the benefits that I have enjoyed as a result of journaling. I have been an avid journal-writer since I could hold a pen, and, although my journaling has changed shape, and improved as my ability improved, the essence of journaling has stayed the same, providing me with a clear representation of myself, my feelings and the events in my life, which I could use to both reflect and take action from. I can honestly say, without my journaling practice I would not be where I am today, having enjoyed two successful careers and feeling professionally and personally satisfied with my life.

I started my career as a personal trainer, before becoming a counselor, which I have now been for the last ten years. Although the move from personal trainer to counselor might be seen as a total career change, from an active, fast paced job to a much more considered and sedentary one, I see it as simply shifting the way I work with people, and help them grow. It might be surprising, but I have used journaling as a key tool throughout both my careers. When I first began as a physical trainer I encouraged my clients to keep records of the exercises they did outside of our sessions, as well as the food they were fueling their bodies with. As I learnt more about journaling, the records I asked them to keep began to evolve into journals similar to those I discuss here. When I became a counselor, the journaling process I had created evolved again to focus more on mental health and understanding unhealthy thought processes.

Journaling is often thought of as something to improve your mental outlook, or help with unpleasant feelings, and, while this is definitely true, journaling is also about achievement. You can use your journal to set goals, and document your path towards them, making it a perfect tool for self improvement of all sorts, including physical improvement.

In fact, these two outcomes, increased positive mental strength and accomplishing goals, are intertwined. As I discussed at the beginning of this introduction, feeling frustrated and negative about yourself and your abilities can cause you to retreat into yourself and away from opportunities, convinced that you would not be able to succeed in new situations. Working on your self-esteem and increasing your confidence will allow you to seize these opportunities and work towards achieving your goals, whether short term or long term. Conversely, accomplishing something you've been working towards, or even putting a concrete plan in place that will help you reach your goal, can boost your sense of self-esteem exponentially. It doesn't have to be a massive achievement, as even taking small steps towards a goal can fill you with a sense of purpose, lifting your self-confidence and overall mental health. You can think of journaling as a "buy one get one free" deal, giving you both of these outcomes at once. This works by giving you significant insight into your thoughts and feelings, what decisions you have made and why you have acted as you have. Having this information opens up your options for the future, as you can take control and implement your plans with full knowledge of what you want and how to work with yourself, and with others, to achieve your goals.

Over the course of my career, I have seen many of my clients blossom through the art of journaling into confident, self-aware individuals who are capable of making and executing clear plans for their life goals. One client felt stuck in her job, working long hours in a field she had little interest in, which left her exhausted and with little time to spend on her interests. This was negatively affecting her mood, and she came to me for counselling as a result. She wanted help regulating her emotions, and putting coping mechanisms in place to boost her mood. While journaling proved an incredibly effective tool in her emotional toolbox, it also propelled her to make concrete changes in her life. Once she had a record of how she spent her days, she was able to then use that to carve out time for herself, making an effort to reconnect with hobbies she had previously enjoyed, such as crafting. She realised how much enjoyment crafting brought her, and made it a personal goal to move towards a job in that industry, which would improve her job satisfaction and her mental health. She now runs her own successful company making crafting kits. Her trajectory towards success and happiness is not unusual, and is echoed by many more clients I have worked with. Many personal training clients, who came to me simply for help with their physical fitness, also went on to make changes in their lives outside of losing weight or gaining muscle as a result of their experience journaling, such as changing careers, moving countries and meeting new partners.

You can experience the same change in mindset and personal growth as my clients have, I promise you. With this book, I wanted to expand my client list and help more people, including anyone who has ever felt stuck or frustrated in their life, including you. With these skills and tools, you will be able to take your life to the next level, doing things you never thought possible, or that others previously prevented you from doing. The rest of your life can change, becoming an exciting journey of personal growth. So why wait?

Growth happens all the time, incrementally, and with this book you have the power to immediately start to change your patterns of growth from bad habits to better ones. It can feel hard to change your behaviour at first, as so many of our actions are built up over time, and ingrained into our routines.

Although you might feel as if your thoughts are constantly changing, it is very easy to get sucked into patterns of negative thoughts, which can prevent you from moving forward. Self-awareness can sometimes be uncomfortable, as it presents us with a clear picture of our strengths and flaws, and often our brain reacts to hide this awareness, aiming to keep us from experiencing this discomfort. However, gradually we can build up our comfort with our own self, and use this awareness to work on aspects of ourselves we wish to change, and use our strengths to achieve our desires. Journaling is the perfect space for this process of increasing self-awareness, as it provides a safe environment for you to learn about yourself with total honesty and without any fear of judgement.

Both the benefits of journaling I have observed at work and in my research can be yours, and each chapter of this book will take you further on the journey to a new, self-aware and confident version of yourself. As well as providing an overview of the history and philosophy of journaling, introducing you to the ranks of successful journal writers through time, I will also take you step by step through the practicalities of how to begin your journal, including how to make it an integral part of your daily life. There is a style of journaling for everyone—perhaps even several—and I will introduce you to a variety of them, so you can find the one that is perfect for you, and what you hope to achieve with your journal.

I have focused on the mental benefits of journaling so far here, and the impact it can have on your life, but I will also take you through the physical benefits you may start to notice as you journal. With this book as your guide, you'll gain the ability to work confidently and successfully towards any goal you want, reaching your maximum potential.

CHAPTER 1

THE LOW-DOWN

We've discussed some of the benefits of journaling that I have personally experienced and witnessed, and how the process of journaling works in tandem to improve your outlook and help you become more proactive, helping you achieve your goals. But what exactly is journaling? And where does it come from?

Although we will look at the definition of a journal, exploring how it might differ from other forms of record, like the diary, do not worry about getting stuck in a rigid routine of record keeping. The flexibility of the journal form, and its ability to adapt to your needs, is what makes it such a valuable tool. Your journey is personal to you, so the tools you need to travel it will also be personal to you.

I will then look into the past of the journal, looking at how it has developed and changed over time, to give you a sense of the wealth of tradition and history you are now part of as a journal writer. Naturally, with such a personal medium, there is also a personal history of the journal. I will take you through important historical figures who wrote a journal, exploring the full breadth of what you can achieve with this technique. However, journaling is of course a living breathing changing form, and there are many modern celebrities and other successful people who attribute their journey to journaling. With this overview of the form and personal histories behind it, you will feel grounded in the tradition of journal writers, with a solid base with which to start your own journey.

The Definition of a Journal

The most common definition of a journal is that it is some form of written record kept by a person about their life, recording the events of each day, and sometimes their feelings about these events. This is what most of us will have in mind when we think about journaling, and it does encompass a range of the different techniques people use to journal. However, even this broad definition is flexible, and can be changed to suit your needs.

One point of flexibility is the reference to recording each day. You might have read the definition and wondered about the similarity to the definition of a diary. These two forms are often used interchangeably, but there are subtle differences between them. A diary is a daily record of the events of your day, and, as such, frequently forms part of your wider journal project. However, a journal is more dynamic than a static record of events, as it functions as an active place to work through and process your thoughts and feelings. While a diary is primarily focused on the past, a journal uses the lessons of the past to look to the future, planning the steps needed to achieve your goals and make your future the present.

The journal is a record of your mind in action, based on the self-awareness you have gained from seeing your life clearly. This self-awareness is built up through the diary-like recording of your life in motion, allowing you to see where changes can be made, but the sense of forward motion and achievement a journal gives you is what makes it a different form. The fact that a diary is often incorporated into the journal form does give you a sense of its adaptability. Your journal can include whatever you want to include—a habit tracker, a meal plan, visual elements like collage or photographs—as long as you feel that these tools help you to focus on your life and your goals.

Journaling Up Until Today

Discussing the history of journaling is not intended to scare you away from it, but to give you a sense of the long tradition of journaling, and the wealth of successful historical figures that used journaling as a tool. These famous figures are now your peers. You are a journal writer just like they were, and you should be proud to take your place amongst their ranks. This overview of the history of journaling is to welcome you in, and give you a glimpse of the tradition you are now part of, and the value it has brought to generations of people.

The Timeline of the Journal

The journal is, as any written record, a more fragile object, easily damaged or erased, and so for each example of historical journaling we are lucky to still have today, we can assume there are thousands of thousands more that have been destroyed by time. Even so, the history of journaling can be charted back for millennia, demonstrating the vitality of this art to the human race.

One of the earliest examples of a journal stretches back almost 2,000 years to Ancient China, with a man's daily record of his journey to perform an offering for the Emperor at the Mount Tai mountain. In a society where the Emperor was the only source of truth and official history, Ma Dubo's diary is a valuable record of how ordinary Chinese people were living, working and thinking at that time.

In a similar vein, the journal of Michitsuna no Haha ("Michitsuna's mother" in Japanese) from Japan in 974 A.D. gives us the daily life and perspective of a woman in the Japanese Heian Court, which is incredibly valuable given how rare women's voices are within history. The unnamed woman kept a detailed account of not only her actions but also her emotions, describing her loneliness at court, her grief at her mother's death, and celebrating the successes of her son in various contests.

Journaling was not limited to ordinary people however. We also have accounts from emperors and other distinguished rulers, that give us a personal insight not only into the details of their rule, but how they thought about leadership and what they prioritised. The Roman Emperor Marcus Aurelius filled twelve books' worth of journals between 167 A.D. and 180 A.D., translated as "Things to One's Self," and known as his "Meditations" today. Although these early examples do all tie in with our modern conceptions of journals, in that they cover personal accounts of events, thoughts and feelings, there is one important difference between these and the journals we keep today. Historically, diary keeping was a form of public record, and often intended for public consumption. Michitsuna no Haha, for example, intended her journal to be read by other women at court, and form a bridge of connection between them.

The shift from public recordkeeping to private rumination is difficult to pinpoint exactly, but many historians think it started to change in the 17th century, and point to Samuel Pepys as one of the first to keep a private diary. Pepys's diary is perhaps one of the most famous historical diaries, spanning ten years of his life and over a million words. These ten years, 1659-1669 encompass important historical events such as the Great

Fire of London, the plague and the ascension of King Charles II to the throne, as well as more personal details such as his household, his finances and even his affairs with actresses. Due to these potentially incriminating details, he guarded the privacy of his diary fiercely, and even wrote in code on some occasions, demonstrating the shift towards the modern conception of the journal as "for your eyes only."

Although travel diaries had been popular throughout history, in the 18th century journals became a more creative pursuit, used by writers and artists such as Kafka and Tolstoy. With the rise of modern warfare, especially trench warfare, the war journal became more common.

Although no doubt the journal writers felt the mental benefits of journal keeping, the explicit recognition of the therapeutic potential of journals really started in the 1960s, with psychologist Dr. Ira Progoff's Intensive Journal Method classes. 1978 marks the publication of three landmark books about journaling and personal development, including one by Dr. Progoff. Journaling found its way into the educational system, and then with the rise of social media, onto the internet. This is almost a return to the historic conception of journaling as a form of public record, as blogging, vlogging and social media websites like Instagram are designed to share your thoughts with other people. The public nature of internet journals is why they will largely not be covered in this book, as I believe the private nature of the journal is what creates that safe space, and allows you to be fully honest with yourself.

Historical Journal Writers

Many of these historical journal writers are only well-known as a result of their journals surviving and becoming useful historical documents. Ma Dubo and Michitsuna no Haha, for example, are only known to us because we have their diaries, and even then we don't know Michitsuna no Haha's proper name, only the names of others she wrote down. Samuel Pepys did have a successful career within the naval government, but again is most famous for his unfailing record of time.

However, if we change focus, and look not at famous journals, but at famous individuals, we can see that many important historical figures also kept journals, to varying degrees of privacy. This is certainly true of Marcus Aurelius, who, when writing his journal, was the most powerful man in the world, due to the expanse and affluence of the Roman Empire he commanded. His journal combines his own meditations about leadership and success with sections of Stoic philosophy, giving us an insight into how he led, and what he took inspiration from. The importance of journaling to the Emperor can be clearly seen, as he took the time to write this journal while in a tense and dangerous situation, the front lines of war with Germania.

The connection between leadership and journaling can be seen again in Benjamin Franklin, a talented polymath and one of the Founding Fathers of the United States. A scientist, inventor, statesman, printer, and politician, Franklin left a long legacy of achievements behind him. How did he do it all? There is no doubt he was naturally intelligent and talented, but one clue to his success lies in his journaling. He created a program of self-improvement based on thirteen moral principles, and recorded his attempts to live by these in his journal, noting each failure, and reflecting on the achievements of each day. He prompted himself with the question "What good shall I do this day?" and kept to a strict schedule in order to achieve his aims. These are all variations on journal writing techniques you can implement for yourself, and I will take you through how to do so further on in the book.

It's not just political leaders and heads of state that have used journaling to achieve their goals, but also leaders in a range of different fields. Journal writing in the sciences may have a slightly different form to Franklin's program of self-improvement, more commonly collections of notes and preliminary calculations, but they still show the importance of having a personal space for the mind to work on problems. The famous physicist Albert Einstein's notebooks, for example, range from doodled sketches and quick mathematical games and puzzles, to calculations and notes for what would later be his theory of relativity in his Zurich notebook, completed in

1912-13. Einstein's notes, over 80,000 pages of them, are a valuable record of the thought process of an incredibly intelligent man, showing his own brilliance, but also his ability to collaborate and consider other people's ideas.

Significant scientific theories and ideas can frequently be traced back to notes in a journal, and this is as true of evolution as it is of relativity. Charles Darwin was a frequent diary writer, making observations throughout his travels, and speculating about connections between natural phenomena. In these notebooks we can see the first sketch of an evolutionary tree, as well as the beginnings of the theory of natural selection and *The Origin of Species*.

Leonardo da Vinci is another polymath, whose notebooks combine anatomical studies, mechanical engineering, drawings, clothes inventories and ideas for inventions we use today, such as tanks and water pumps. Leonardo da Vinci was a Renaissance man, famed equally for his scientific and creative achievements, and proof that a journal can shift to accommodate anything you wish to throw at it.

Of course, journaling may seem like a natural extension of creativity for those in the arts industries, and that might explain why quite so many artists, writers and philosophers kept a journal. Mark Twain, the famous American writer, kept a journal from the age of 21, filling 50 notebooks through the course of his life with observations and thoughts that can be traced into his published work. Anais Nin valued journaling so highly that she saw her notebooks as her best work, above her published essays and fiction, while Ernest Hemingway kept a detailed account of his entire life, relying on his journals to make sense of his thoughts and organize his life. Artists used their journals to guide them through the difficult and uncontrollable process of creativity and inspiration, and this steadiness is a benefit anyone, not just those in creative industries, can benefit from.

The Benefits of Journaling

The previous sections have touched on some of the benefits experienced by successful journal writers from the past, and have hopefully given you a sense of the value and breadth of the tradition you are now a part of. I now want to take the history of the journal into the present day, and examine some examples of successful journal writers within our current moment and society, as well as tease out some more of the benefits journal writing has afforded these celebrities, entrepreneurs and sporting champions. These are examples of the most public forms of achievement you can attain using journaling, but quieter, more private successes are equally important, and I will take you through a few testimonies of personal attainment from my clients, and draw out from these success stories what you can expect to gain from your journaling project.

Successful Journal Writers

As the history of journaling suggests, journal writing has only grown in popularity through the centuries, and the success stories of the past continue into the present. Uncovering the routines and journeys of successful, rich and famous people frequently reveals a journaling habit in some form or another, once again revealing the importance journaling can play in focusing the mind towards bigger and brighter goals, allowing you to quickly ascend to the top of your field. Many Hollywood actors are also Hollywood journal writers, using their journals to keep track of their emotions and trajectories through a high-strung and changeable industry. Jennifer Aniston, one of the stars of the beloved sitcom *Friends*, began acting at a young age, simultaneously beginning her journaling career. She reportedly has kept a journal since she was 13, considering them a form of therapy, which allows her to work through her emotions on the page, and ensures she can save the drama for the big screen!

Another journal convert, and former child star, is Emma Watson, who has also journaled for years. Emma outlined her journaling process in an interview, describing the various types of journal she keeps, including ones for dreams, advice, yoga, acting work and even observations about people she meets. Emma clearly appreciates the flexibility of the journal, allowing you to keep track of multiple areas of your life, although when you come to start your journal, you can choose whether to follow Emma into a multiple journal project, or streamline into one journal for ease of access.

Journaling appears in the lives of successful businessmen, as well as actors and other creative stars. Steve Jobs, one of the co-founders of Apple Inc., which is now ranked as one of the largest technology companies and the world's most valuable brand, started every day with a form of reflective meditation that echoes journal prompts. He revealed he started every day by asking himself, "If today was the last day of my life, would I want to do what I am about to do today?" and using his response as a guide to how he felt his life was proceeding, and taking inspiration to change if the answer was repeatedly "no."

Although Jobs spent his five reflective minutes in front of the bathroom mirror as opposed to in front of a journal, the principle of taking time to consider the day, and life, ahead, is the same in journal writing. John Paul DeJoria, the billionaire founder of brands like Patron tequila and Paul Mitchell haircare, has a similarly reflective practice. He spends the first five minutes awake each morning checking in with himself, finding a sense of calm and certainty that lasts throughout the day. These busy business leaders prioritised their routine of reflection, signalling just how valuable they found them as tools to help them perform at the very top of their game.

Testimonies

So far I have taken you through the journaling habits of very publicly successful people, whether historical figures, Hollywood film stars, business giants or billionaires, but this should not intimidate you. Journaling is for everyone, no matter what your goals are. If your desires for your life include fame or extreme wealth, these examples should act as a spur to you, demonstrating the possibilities of high profile success that can be achieved. However, if your conception of success is a life under the public radar, with more personal and private achievements, journal writing is still the tool for you. You might also find that as you focus on your life, and begin to advance in the areas you want to, that your dreams will change and grow, no longer limited by unfavorable circumstances or even your own self-belief.

I have already discussed one of my clients' experiences with this: how she started journaling as a tool to help her mental health, and used it to change her life and start her own business. I want to now take you through the experience of one of my personal training clients, who had only come to me to improve his general fitness, and through the skills he gained working with me, improved his whole life.

Alan, we'll call him, was a mid-thirties IT consultant, working in customer support, who wanted personal training because he had been warned the combination of a sedentary desk job, a lack of exercise and an unhealthy diet could lead to heart issues if nothing changed. As I always do, I asked him to keep a journal for a week, to get a sense of how he lived his life, and where we could make time for his exercise plan. Examining his life in such detail was the first push towards total self-awareness he had experienced, and we made a list of changes to implement slowly, such as waking up earlier to exercise before work, and setting one day aside to meal prep.

Sticking to this plan, Alan was quickly becoming healthier and healthier, gaining muscle and feeling much more active. He also expressed to me how taking this time to take care of himself, and keeping a record of it, was improving his sense of self-worth, devalued by years of demoralising customer service work. He was now aware of the value of his mind and body, and from treating himself with respect, began to demand more from others. Although my sessions with Alan came to an end, he got in touch a number of years later to thank me. Provoked by the journaling system I had recommended, his increased determination and self-respect had led him on a journey, leaving the IT company first to travel the world, then to start his own company in a beautiful holiday destination, offering unique travel experiences to other tourists, and then to start a family, having met a like-minded soul on his travels. Journaling pushed him to consider his life clearly, and to ask what more he could be experiencing. Alan's testimony was one of the ones that sparked me to write this book, as I felt so strongly that the power he had gained through journaling should be made available and easily accessible to anyone who needed it.

What Does This Mean for You?

Now that you have a sense of the history of journaling, you can begin to appreciate the wealth of tradition and experience in the field. You can rest reassured that no matter how or what you want to use your journal for, there either be a previous writer you can take inspiration from, or a range of writers you can draw from to create your own original journal. I hope this chapter has also given you a sense of the value of journal writing, which has meant so much to so many throughout history. You may have also begun to sense how keeping a journal can improve your life, having seen the success stories of Steve Jobs, Benjamin Franklin, Jennifer Aniston and my client Alan, and how the focus journaling brings them allows them to set their ambitions higher and higher, enjoying wholly successful lives.

CHAPTER 2

HOW TO JOURNAL TODAY

The information in Chapter One has given you a sense of the depth of experience and knowledge around journal writing and its benefits, and how established it is as a practice. In this chapter, we're going to dive in, and focus on the practicalities of journaling. Not only will I take you through what journaling is, and begin to suggest some techniques and methods for you to use, but I will also set you up with the correct preparation for beginning your journaling adventure. You might have already tried to start journaling, but found it difficult to keep up, or struggled to find a time that suited you. These are all issues we will consider, as they are some of the biggest stumbling blocks to an enjoyable and sustainable journaling experience. Preparation is the key to success, and creating a solid journaling process now, that accurately reflects your life, will support you to make part of your daily routine, and as vital to you as it is to the celebrities and businessmen we looked at in Chapter One. If you are feeling frustrated with your life, or your self-esteem is low, starting a journal without considering all the factors can become self-sabotaging, causing you to quickly slip out of the routine, and perhaps do more damage to your sense of self-worth. It is important to note however that once you have this routine in place, you may find it changes naturally as changes occur in your life—do not worry about this, as once you have made journaling a foundation stone of your life it can easily adapt to your circumstances.

Choosing When to journal

The first step is deciding what time you will dedicate to journaling. Although this might be impacted by your schedule, and we will discuss that in the next section, here I want you to focus on what you would like to get out of your journaling practice, as certain aims you have might be more aligned with morning intention-setting, or evening reflection. This can also be affected by what kind of person you are, and when you work best. If you are a morning person by nature, you might find journaling in the morning complements your routine, and enhances your productivity even further. If you are a night owl, you might find you naturally have time in the evening to dedicate to your journal writing. However, as with all aspects of journaling, these are not concrete rules, and should be seen more as suggestions for you to consider. You might find that the opposite is true, and that although you work best in the morning, you enjoy taking time in the evening to journal, or that if you function better at night, journaling pushes you to enjoy the mornings more than you usually do, and start your day off on a more purposeful note.

When you choose to journal can align itself with what type of journaling practice you wish to employ, or even which technique you want to focus on at this present moment. As I outline some of the morning and evening systems for you to consider, if one of these practices calls to you as you're reading, then try following it to see whether it will work for you. Although journaling is an aspirational project, try to also think realistically about whether it will really work for you, using the other advice in this chapter.

We have briefly touched on morning journal writers, those like Steve Jobs who use prompts to set their intentions for today. They use their time to think critically about the day ahead, and put in place clear goals they can refer back to throughout the day. This can be an effective way to live intentionally, and keep each day focused on working towards your larger goals.

Conversely, morning journaling can also be a way to clear your mind of any underlying stresses before tackling the day. You can use your journal as a "brain dump" for your thoughts, acting as a cleanse. This can be done simply through writing in a "stream of consciousness" mode, simply putting any thought you have on paper, or by setting parameters for your morning writing. Julia Cameron coined the idea of "morning pages," three pages written each and every morning (Ye, 2019). By forcing yourself to write a certain amount, you start flexing your mental muscles, while cleansing yourself of any past worries or thoughts you don't need to take with you into the day. You might also find that while you were asleep, your brain has been subconsciously ruminating on any problems you might have, and that a solution might be found in your morning journal entry.

The concept of mental cleansing is also an essential function of evening journaling, as it allows you to reflect on the day and put it to bed, before you yourself go to bed. Here, you can purge any stressful situations you encountered that day, and ensure that you aren't carrying any tension into the next day. If you have issues sleeping, perhaps caused by worry, you might also find that writing in a journal before bedtime as part of a set nighttime routine helps calm your thoughts, and help you get a better night's sleep.

Reflecting on your day will also give you the opportunity to analyse the events that took place and your actions. You might be able to identify areas where you can make changes, or congratulate yourself on your behaviour, or track your progress towards your long term goals. Journaling at the end of the day does not just have to be about reflection however, and often thoughts about the present will inevitably inspire you to consider the future. You might want to set your intentions for the day the night before, so you can wake up with a clear sense of purpose for your day, and be able to jump straight into action.

You also do not necessarily have to journal at the end of the day, if you already have a nighttime routine you cannot accommodate journaling into, but you could take the end of your work day, for example, as a time to reflect on the work you achieved that day, and set goals for the next, giving yourself a clear separation between work and home. You might take after dinner as the end of your day, and spend some time then working on your journal—with the added benefit of aiding your digestion! There are many options to choose from when it comes to integrating journaling into your life, and if one time slot does not work, try and pay attention to where your mind is telling you is best for you.

Making Space for Journaling

You might have a clear journaling time in mind after reading the previous section, but when you try it you find it frequently gets interrupted by other demands on your time. Or you might be unable to even think of a section of free time you could dedicate to journaling, and feel demoralised about even starting. It can be hard at first, as it is with any new activity, to adjust your schedule to include journaling, especially if you already lead a busy life, whether by choice or necessity. But there are methods you can use to integrate journaling into your routines, and you might find once you start journaling that your schedule frees up, as you become more intentional with your time.

Finding Time in a Busy World

Intentionality is a fundamental part of the journaling process. The intention you put into creating and following through on your journal writing process is given back to you, as you become more intentional with your time, and are able to prioritise activities that bring you happiness, as well as taking you closer to your goals. You will have to be intentional with your practice at first, deliberately carving out time for this new life practice.

To start this process, you might want to keep a log of the next week of your life, creating an honest account of each hour of your day. With this, you can see where you are sending your precious time and attention, and where changes can be made. There might be obvious gaps in your schedule, where you can simply slot in time to journal, but if not, you might have to look harder to carve out time. Can you wake up earlier, either to journal, or to give yourself journaling time later in the day? Could you go to bed slightly later, and journal then? If you cannot give yourself more time, then it's time to get intentional about the time you have. Are there chunks of time you spend aimlessly checking emails, on social media, or watching television? All of these are perfectly adequate activities, but if they are not done with intention, they can quickly begin to suck time from your day. Can you set yourself a limit on your phone or computer, and use some of that time gained back to journal? Can you decide to watch one or two episodes of a television show, but resolve not to flick between channels, or binge watch?

Remember, journaling is also an enjoyable activity you have chosen to do, and that will hopefully not only help you achieve your goals, but also be an activity you take pleasure in doing. Therefore, reducing your other leisure activities to incorporate time to journal does not mean you are losing any leisure time, but just rearranging it to better suit your needs.

Creating Solitude for Yourself

Although journaling is a leisure activity, it does differ in one key way from other leisure activities you might enjoy, in that it should be done in as close to complete solitude as possible. This might mean in order to journal, you have to rearrange or cancel social events until you have finalised your journal writing routine, and have found the way to balance time alone with time spent with friends. You do not have to isolate yourself completely from social interaction, but once again just think intentionally about how you are spending your time, and how you can carve out a little time for yourself. Journaling requires you to focus on yourself, and to be completely honest, and in order to make this process of honesty as painless and easy as possible for you, it is best done privately, creating a truly safe space for yourself. It might not be possible to journal totally alone, if you take care of young children for example, or have other obligations, but if this is the case please rest assured that you do not have to sacrifice the sanctity of journal writing. In its flexibility, journaling is here to work for you, in service of your needs, and compromises can always be made.

If there is no way you can make time to write in solitude, can you at least ensure that your journal is for your eyes only, and that yours is the only voice written in it? Treating your personal journal with respect is an extension of treating yourself with respect, and the choices you make with respect. If you can write in solitude, try to make sure you're not distracted by other tasks, and can give your full attention to your thoughts, and the process of writing. I have referred to "solitude" throughout this section, and I want to clarify how this differs from simply being alone. You are perhaps alone when doing household chores, such as cleaning, or laundry, but this is not solitude. Solitude is intentional time spent alone, engaged in conversation with yourself, and not distracted by other tasks, and journaling is one of the key ways to reach this state. Through journaling in solitude, you will begin to develop and flex your self-awareness, and get comfortable with yourself.

The benefits of solitude and journaling are intertwined, as the self-acceptance you will gain through both can help you to find more happiness in your life, experience less and cope better with stress, and even alleviate any deeper struggles with your mental health you may have.

Turning Journaling Into a Habit

Once you have found the best time to journal, considering all the factors mentioned above, the next step is to turn it into a consistent part of your routine. Creating new habits can be a difficult process, and it is easy to get discouraged once you miss a few days in a row, and start to doubt that journaling is really for you. Do not take any missteps personally, as this is a common problem that can easily be resolved. I am going to give you some tips and tricks I have learned throughout my careers that will help you cement journal writing as a habit. If you try these, and are still unable to commit to daily journaling, you might want to reconsider the journaling time you have decided on. If it is too difficult to squeeze it into the time slot you have set aside for writing, it might be best to change when you intend to journal. Starting a journal is a process, and it might take attempting a few different ways and times for you to find the method that really works for you.

Habits form over time. Beating yourself up for not being perfect at journaling a week into the process is unnecessary, and is only going to make you associate journaling with negative emotions and failure.

Instead, resolve to start small. Do not make any other big changes in your life during this adjustment period. Once you have started journaling, this will give you the self-confidence and capability to change your life in a calm and focused manner, giving you the best chance of success.

If you are feeling overwhelmed, break the process down into smaller chunks. For example, you could start by simply spending five minutes writing down how you feel every day. Keeping the commitment small at the start means that you are more likely to achieve it, and this sense of success can spur you on to further achievements. These other achievements could be increasing the time you spend journaling, or starting to use it with more intention, such as setting future plans and goals. You might also find that even though you have only committed to five minutes, journaling can be addictive, and that you want to continue once your five minutes are up, reinforcing it as a positive habit you enjoy.

Keeping it small at the start will help you commit, but if you're still missing a day or two with the low stakes, don't beat yourself up. Accept that this is part of a process, and remind yourself that even if you miss a day or two, that's still five or six days spent journaling, which is better than none. Challenging negative thoughts can be hard, but an easy way to do it is to immediately counter any with a "but" statement. "I forgot to journal today" then becomes "I forgot to journal today, but I did yesterday, and I will remember tomorrow," reminding you of your past success, and keeping you focused on your long term goal.

The best way to form a habit is to start small, but go long. Having a long adjustment period means that the habit is much more likely to have become part of your routine, and something you expect to do each day. Experts agree that doing a new activity for at least 30 days gives it the best chance of becoming a habit (Young, 2017). You can make it easy for yourself by starting at the beginning of a month, and taking the whole month as a training period for yourself. During this training period, you should plan to write in your journal every day. Not only will this give you a clear idea of your activities, your mood and your thoughts, both about starting journaling and about future goals you would like to achieve, it also provides the sense of consistency that is vital to habit forming.

If the thought of 30 days fills you with dread, I have some easy techniques that can help you to keep going. If you have trouble remembering your commitment, or find that you are highly motivated for one week before tapering off, set reminders on your phone to prompt you to journal. This does not have to be a long term solution, but for this initial adjustment period it can be useful to have a physical reminder to keep yourself on track. You can also do this by scheduling your journaling to coincide with a trigger activity, that should hopefully prompt you to journal. If you decide to journal after a meal, once you have eaten, you might then instinctively look for your journal, as you will have trained yourself to associate eating breakfast or dinner with journaling. You can also trigger yourself by leaving your journal in a clearly visible place—a brightly colored one often works best for this, as the sight of the journal will then remind you to use it.

Because a month is a long period of time, you can also break it up, and reward yourself along the way, to reinforce journal writing as a positive habit for you. Again, start small to encourage yourself to continue. Reward yourself for your first streak of consecutive days, then for a week, then for two, and so on. Eventually you will come to feel that journaling itself is a reward for you, but until that point, treat yourself with little rewards for succeeding in creating a solid habit.

Writing Your Journal

Before we get into the finer detail of what to write in your journal, I just want to briefly touch on the actual physical journal you use. Our increasingly digital and online world can mean that you don't have a physical journal or notebook ready at home to use, and before buying the journal that is going to change your life, there are of course some points you should take into account. There are a range of journals out there, from plain notebooks to planners to bullet journals to pre-made prompt and gratitude journals, and you can easily be seduced into buying an expensive but beautiful journal that promises to transform you. The process of journaling will change your life, but only if you give it the power to. The focus should be on how your journal can work for you, not how you can fit yourself to a template, and so I recommend that until you know how you like to journal, and what you need your journal to give you, start with a plain notebook. This way you can explore any technique you want, through any medium you want, and find what works best for you. Then, armed with this knowledge, you can return to the stationary aisle, and get a more structured journal if that feels like it will fit with your style. Even with a plain notebook, try to get one that appeals to you visually, as it will help you associate journaling with positive emotions, and help you form the habit.

Now that you have your journal, what will you write in it? This section will take you through what to include in your journal, while Chapter Four will go into more detail on how to record these things, and the different techniques you can use. The foundation of your journal should be some form of daily log, especially at the beginning of your journal writing journal. You might have already begun keeping one to see where you could carve out time to journal, and keeping a record of your schedule can be a useful place to start. You can do this in as little or as much detail as you like, so long as it gives you a clear picture of the events that take place each week. This schedule might work in tandem with other daily actions you wish to record, such as your sleeping patterns, meals or exercise.

Here though, it is important to keep in mind the difference between a diary and a journal that we discussed in Chapter One. A journal is an active place of thought and reflection, and so recording things like your sleep, or what food you eat, should be accompanied by a note of the effect they had on you, both physically and emotionally. A diary captures the bare bones of your schedule, and knows that you've had a busy day, but a journal knows whether it was a productive day, where you felt in control of your workload and commitments, or a frustrating day, where you were pulled into irrelevant meetings, and felt like you were wasting your time.

The extra information you'll gather through your journaling, can then be turned into action. There are many different levels of action you can take from your journal, and you can combine them, or use them as stepping stones to make major changes. The first level is gaining control of your schedule. Once you can see clearly how you're spending your time each day, you can see areas that are not working as well as they should, and time you feel like you're wasting. Set your new schedule in your journal with intention, focusing on the activities you need and want to do, and eliminating those that do not serve you.

Like a scientist in a laboratory, you can experiment, making notes of what works and what doesn't in your journal, moving you closer and closer to your ideal life. The sense of self-awareness and control you will gain from this process may spur you on to further levels of action. You might become aware of gaps in your life, or achievements you want to reach, but are unsure how. Your journal gives you a place to work this out, and you can start by writing your goal at the top of the page, and simply listing the steps you need to take, or even how to find out what you'll need to do, as well as any worries or concerns you might have. From this you can form a plan of action, and methodically working through the steps should alleviate any fears you have about pushing yourself. You can record your progress, and any issues you encounter on your path can be solved within the journal. This method works for both goals you wish to achieve and problems you wish to solve, and you will soon find that your problems get smaller, while your goals get bigger and bigger.

Making physical change in your life, whether that's implementing an exercise plan, solving a problem at work, or overhauling your entire career, will naturally create mental and emotional changes for you. You might feel less worry, or more confident, as a result of the steps you take to solve your problems and progress your life. Physical goals, such as improving your fitness, or making the effort to cook more often, will also have an impact on how you feel. However, you can enhance these effects, and focus on them, using your journal. There are two ways to do this, and you will probably find that a combination of both works for you, depending on the needs of your emotions at the time.

The first is an extension of the problem-solving journaling you have been doing, but focusing on emotional issues rather than physical ones. If something at work has upset us, or we've had a conversation with a friend or family member that has left us feeling hurt or uncomfortable, common outlets we might use are to lash out instinctively and immediately, or to retreat inwards, and keep our hurt and frustration bottled up. Neither of these outlets are really outlets, in the sense of a healthy and productive way to express our feelings. Lashing out can often backfire, inflaming the situation and leaving you with regrets about how you handled yourself, while bottling up your emotions can stunt your relationships, and leave resentment festering. Journaling can provide a healthy outlet, as it allows you to express your feelings in private. You have a safe space to work through the event, releasing your frustration without fear of retribution from others and learning what you can say in future situations to express yourself respectfully, calmly and honestly.

The second way to improve your emotional stability and strength is to focus on the positives of your day, that you might have missed at the time. Gratitude journaling has become increasingly popular, as appreciating what you have can also improve your view of the future. Writing down what you are grateful for each day, whether one thing or five, can force you to reassess your life and improve your mood just as much as journaling for achievement can.

Journal prompts

Many gratitude journals you can buy are based on a form of prompt journaling, either asking you to list what you are grateful for that day, or requiring a certain number of gratitude statements, whether that is the best thing to happen today, or five things today that you are grateful for. Using a prompt like this can be useful to get you started, as it takes away the fear of the wide open blank journal page and focuses your thoughts on a question. Of course, if you do use a prompt, you do not have to stop writing once you have answered the question, and you might find that once you have started writing, more things you want to say pop up, outside the limits of the prompt. You might realise that by starting your journal with a description of your day each time, you are prompting yourself. Or that by using dinner as a trigger to journal, you start each entry with a description of the meal, prompted by your trigger. These are indirect prompts, and they can be just as useful as more overt questions.

One area where a direct prompting question does help is that of emotion, and your deeper thoughts and feelings. It can be tough to understand the complexities of your emotions as you experience them, especially if they are intense or negative emotions, and a prompting question is often a good way to start that conversation with yourself, and tease out the layers of what you are feeling, and why. This can lead to some of the more action-focused journaling I outlined in the previous section, as once you understand your feelings, you can take action on them. In fact, using a prompt can be wholly about taking action, rather than exploring emotion. Benjamin Franklin's question, What good shall I do on this day?" prompted him to create action in his life, and do good deeds (McKay, 2014). You can use a direct prompt like this, asking yourself questions like "What three tasks can I accomplish today?" or "What exercise can I do today?" or make use of a more subtle one. A prompt about your favourite activity could inspire you to schedule in time to do more of it, or a prompt about your favourite clothing could lead to you reorganizing your wardrobe to include more items you love, giving yourself a makeover and getting rid of anything you no longer wear or like.

Prompts can be a fantastic spark for creativity, lighting the match for the fire inside you. You might find you use them daily, or that you keep a reserve of them for when your usual inspiration runs out, and you need to reignite that spark. Here is a selection of prompts you might want to use:

- What three things are you grateful for today?
- What are you most looking forward to today?
- What do you want your life to look like in five/ten/twenty years?
- What are your short term/long term goals?
- What is important to you?
- What are your favourite things about yourself? How can you make the most of these qualities?
- What do other people say are your best qualities? Do you agree?
- What are your favourite hobbies?
- What new activities do you want to try? Make a list of twelve activities you want to try and assign one to each month to work on completing.
- How would you spend your ideal day? Does it look different in summer than in winter?
- How can you treat yourself with more kindness?
- What would you do with your life if you weren't afraid of failure?

- Who are your role models? Why do you admire them, and what qualities do they have that you could work on developing?

- If you met your role model, what would you want to say to them?

- What do you enjoy doing outside of work? How can you do more of it?

- What communities are you part of? How can you involve yourself in your community, and give back?

- What challenge have you recently overcome?

- What is your next challenge?

- What are your favourite books/clothes/musicians?

- What are you an expert in?

- Is there someone in your life you have, or had, a difficult relationship with? Write them a letter, expressing your feelings.

- What is your evening/morning routine? How does it help you?

- What is the best birthday you've ever celebrated? What made it special?

- What makes you feel safe?

- What are your worst fears? Imagine what would happen if they came true, and how you would cope.

- What are you most worried about this week, and what can you do to alleviate this worry?

- How do you feel when you move your body? What movement (running/walking/dancing . . .) feels best?

- Where would you like to live?

- What opportunities are there in your life right now, and how can you take advantage of them?

- What is your favourite meal? Where were you? Who was there with you? How can you replicate it for yourself this week?

- Imagine your life was being made into a film. What key moments would they show? Who would play you?

- What does your ideal future look like? What could you do to make it possible?

- If you were writing a book about your life, what role would your character take? Would your character be a supportive character? Would your character offer advice or lead the band of heroes? What other roles would they play? What tropes would you associate with them?

My Tips

Although I've given you my tips and tricks for journaling throughout, I want to go over a few key points in this section, to make sure you finish this chapter with all the tools you need to start journaling. I have already stressed the importance of making journaling as close to a daily practice as you can, whether that's in the morning or evening, using a prompt to reflect or creating an action plan for your day. Journaling every day gives you a wealth of information about yourself, and it is important to keep this information well organized, in order to properly utilise it. Keeping your entries in chronological order is one key way of organizing yourself. It gives you a clear sense of where you are, what you are doing and when exactly you're doing it, keeping you on track for professional deadlines and social events, as well as allowing you to track your own personal progress towards your goals. It can be hard to motivate yourself, but having a clear deadline, and even a reward in place, can force you to get working on your self-improvement plans.

Keeping yourself rooted in the passage of time also gives you more information about yourself to use to your advantage. If you are feeling demoralised, you can return to entries when you were motivated and excited, and see what conditions were in place then that are missing now. Perhaps your mood changes with the seasons, or is affected by the weather. Realising that can help you work to minimise any negative impact on your mood and your work, by putting in preventative measures. The more you know about yourself, the more you can work with yourself to achieve your goals, instead of feeling like you're constantly fighting with yourself. Keeping each entry chronological and clearly separated from the previous one helps you keep your journal organized and easy to reference, helping you in the long term.

A journal can be an intense place, if you are not used to the self-examination and reflection it can inspire. You may have noticed that many of the example prompts I gave you ask you to consider the most private parts of your subconscious: your fears, hopes and dreams. It can feel incredibly vulnerable to not only give yourself permission to seriously consider your dreams and anxieties, but to then write them down. This is why I stressed the need for privacy when journaling, to ensure you can create that safe space for your vulnerability.

Our instinct can often be to deflect serious thoughts, or defuse situations with humour, or self-deprecation. I want you to promise to try and override these instincts, and keep your journal as a place for total honesty. It is only by being radically honest with yourself that you'll be able to fully assess your life, and start your journey towards your goals. Writing honestly can be hard to do at first, but as you practice, it will get easier and easier to write with the honesty and respect you deserve, and not settle for less. The intensity of a journal is enhanced further by the fact that it is the only place where you are writing to yourself. Although you might think that we would each be our own best audience, it can actually be an incredibly difficult process to start. You might feel too self-conscious, or that you're not quite sure what you actually have to say to yourself! If this is the case, there are a couple of strategies that might help unblock your voice. Firstly, start small. Add in a sentence or two about how you felt that day, or any worries you have, to your daily log, to build your comfort levels, and increase this as time goes by. Secondly, using a prompt can be really valuable here, as it makes you feel as though you are in conversation with someone else, as well as giving you a topic to use as a springboard. Using these tips will help you start the difficult but valuable conversation with yourself, that you'll reap the benefits from for the rest of your life.

The benefits of journal writing both on your mood and in your life are astounding, and journaling with an intention can have a real tangible effect on your life. You need to keep your long term and short term goals in mind when you journal, to ensure that you're focused on taking the steps you need to in order to achieve them. However, don't just treat journaling as a conveyor belt, where if you put in an entry you'll immediately get out success. The final piece of advice I want to give you in this chapter is to enjoy the process of journaling. Not only will this make you more likely to pick up your pen each day, fully immersing yourself in the experience will make accessing the benefits of journaling much easier and more rewarding.

CHAPTER 3

THE VALUE OF JOURNALING

I have alluded to the benefits of journaling throughout, but in this chapter I want to dig deep into what exactly they are, what you might experience, and the science behind it all. Journaling came to prominence as a field of medical and scientific interest in the 1960s, with the psychologist Dr. Progoff's journal writing classes, and subsequent books on the subject. Journaling was seen as a tool to help solve problems of the mind, such as anxiety or depression, and scientific research began analysing and experimenting with journals firmly along these lines. As journaling made the move into the educational system, teachers had expected it to be a useful learning technique, but were surprised to see the extent of the impact it had on students' moods.

Journaling became a technique anybody could use and benefit from, not just people with clearly defined or diagnosed mental health issues. This might sound familiar to you, and I have already mentioned some of the mental benefits of journal writing, as well as the concrete effect these can have on your life. However you might not expect the range of physical benefits journaling can have. By this, I don't just mean the physical changes that it inspires you to make in your life, but the real physical changes it can make to your body. There is scientific research to suggest that journaling can alleviate the physical effects of stress, as well as assist your immune system and improve organ function (Bailey, 2013). It might sound crazy that writing in a journal everyday can have such a significant impact on your body, but it's true!

Mental Benefits

Let's start by looking at the benefits journaling can bring your mind. You might already be aware of some, and I have mentioned a few, such as boosting self-confidence, reducing stress, and soothing any anxieties or worries, as I've taken you through the history of the journal, why those that use journaling do so, and how to start journaling yourself. This section will therefore focus in more depth on how exactly journaling does this, and what goes on in the brain while journaling, looking at some of the scientific data and research to give us a clearer picture of how journal writing helps the mind.

It might sound redundant to say this, but it is valuable to gain a full appreciation of just how important our minds are. We can often neglect the mind for more pressing or physically painful issues with our bodies, forgetting that the two are necessarily intertwined. Your mind is the foundation for everything you do, and keeping your mind as healthy and happy as possible will have an impact on your quality of life, and what you can accomplish. Creating a strong mental foundation will allow you to weather whatever storms come your way, and to focus clearly on your vision of your ideal life, and what you will do to achieve it. So how exactly does journaling help you create this strong mental foundation?

Metacognition and Thought Access

Due to the reflection and self-analysis inherent in journal writing, it is an important tool to improve our metacognitive thinking, and enhance our critical awareness about ourselves. Metacognition describes the processes we engage when we plan, observe and critique our own performance and understanding—when we think about our thinking, essentially. We engage in metacognitive thinking during specific events, when we think about how to approach a plan, monitor our progress, and assess our successes, but also when we think more generally about who we are.

When you think about how you learn best, or identify when you feel most productive, or have your best thoughts, you are engaging in metacognitive thinking, identifying your strengths and weaknesses, and working on how to improve. These skills are incredibly important, because essentially you are learning how to learn, and how you work best. Knowing about different learning and problem solving strategies means you are more likely to employ them, optimising your performance. Improving your metacognitive skills makes you more self sufficient, as you have the skills to adapt to various situations, and become an active learner. This is also called "writing to learn" (Simmons, n.d.).

As well as adapting to a number of different situations, "writing to learn" can also help you adapt to more difficult or complex situations. Research has shown that without external assistance, your brain is only capable of managing three separate thoughts, or variables at once (Moldoveanu and Martin, 2010). Of course, many situations are more complex than this, either including more variables or with more complex variables to begin with. Metacognition and "writing to learn" are useful here, because they improve your brain's ability. The difficulty you may have juggling separate thoughts, even dropping one or two, is lessened by improvements in your mental strength and coordination, allowing you to juggle complicated situations with interrelated problems easily.

In a study, the researcher Kimberley D. Tanner identifies four broad methods for teaching students the art of metacognitive thinking (Chick, 2013). One of these is keeping a reflective journal, encouraging the students to assess their own thinking process, and evaluate which of their study skills were successful, and what aspects they could improve going forward. Although her study is explicitly within an educational framework, we can see that this process does map onto many experiences we have outside of education. You might be dealing with a complex project at work, or having trouble communicating with a friend or partner. Assessing the situation, and deciding what strategies worked well, can help you feel more confident, as well as work on ways to improve your behaviour.

Although Tanner's other strategies do not mention journaling, they do all echo aspects of journal writing, and could be applied within your journal. She encourages students to assess their knowledge before they begin studying, and here you could assess your mood, or your current situation, before a big challenge, or embarking on a new goal. Students should also practice finding their blindspots and identifying what they do not understand. Again here you can examine any negative feelings you have, or any areas of a plan that need further fleshing out and are causing you uncertainty. Finally, students should not only reflect in their journal at the end of the project, but constantly assess their changing levels of knowledge over time. Recognising how your thoughts change can prompt you to either change your strategies, or reassess what is really necessary to you.

Awareness

Metacognition is a valuable form of increased self-awareness, and as we have discussed, self-awareness is fundamental to journaling, and subsequently to making changes in your life. A study titled "Why People Fail to Recognize Their Own Incompetence" published in 2003 examined people's metacognitive skills and knowledge across a range of disciplines, from hunting to medicine (Chick, 2013). They found that across every field, broadly most people had no idea about their own incompetence, and were unable to identify holes in their knowledge, or social interactions with others. They concluded that if you do not have the intellectual ability to find the right answer, you also lack the ability to tell whether your or others' answers are wrong or right. Improving your metacognitive skills improves your intellectual capacity, and so even if you do not yet know the answer, you can discern ridiculous suggestions from realistic ones.

Although recognising your own areas of weakness can initially be dispiriting, you should see it not as an excavation of all of your negative qualities, but as a foundation for self-acceptance and improvement. No personality trait is inherently negative. As a society we tend to judge traits according to certain standards of social aptitude and professional success, which can mean if you do not fit into a narrow definition of success, or professionalism, you might feel socially inferior or incapable. This is not true, if utilised in the right way, every personality trait can be an asset, and help you succeed. The more you know about yourself and how you learn, the more you can put in place to help yourself. You will also be able to get a clearer sense of your own boundaries. A research study found that those with increased metacognitive skills were more capable of monitoring how prepared they were to begin tasks (Chick, 2013). Instead of loading too much onto their plates, they were able to realistically assess how much work they could take on, leading to patterns of sustained success.

Stress Management

Discussing metacognition and self-awareness has hopefully given you some sense of the value of journaling, especially its value as a form of stress management. Stress management is an umbrella term for a variety of strategies to reduce feelings of stress and prevent you feeling overwhelmed and out of control, and so you might experience many of these other benefits as existing within a feedback loop with stress reduction. Increasing your self-awareness may lead you to gain in confidence, or to realise you are overworking yourself, or not using your time effectively. All of these things can then reduce your levels of stress, and so you might find that while the other sections do not explicitly discuss stress management, they do feed into a wider project of managing and minimising any stresses you are experiencing. Stress also has a high physical impact on the body as well as on the mind, and the separate physical benefits gained from reducing stress will be discussed further on, in our wider examination of the physical effects of journal writing. Here I want to look further into the science behind stress relief, focusing on the impact of stressful events, and how journaling can help you overcome these stressors.

The psychologist and researcher James Pennebaker believes that by journaling about specific stressful events, you can learn to accept them, and come to terms with the impact they have had on your life (Baikie and Wilhelm, 2005). By resolving your feelings around these stressors, you can start to reduce the burden they have placed on you, and move on to bigger and better things. This is true not just of current stressful situations that you might be in the middle of, but also ones throughout your past. Pennebaker was part of the first ever study about "expressive writing," a form of journaling (Baikie and Wilhelm, 2005). In the study, some participants were asked to write about the worst experiences in their lives, while a control group wrote about mundane things, like their clothing or their bedroom. Each participant wrote for fifteen minutes for four straight days. They were then assessed objectively four months later, as well as filling out a self-assessment questionnaire. Those that had written about their traumatic experiences reported significant positive changes in their health, and were assessed as having the same. They visited the doctor less than the control group, and took fewer sick days from work. The study therefore concluded that writing about traumatic experiences actually improved long term health, decreasing the impact of health problems. This basic conclusion has not changed in over 20 years of research into expressive writing, and once again highlights the importance of journaling, as opposed to diary entries.

Although not every entry in your journal has to be plumbing the depths of your emotions, braving these deep waters will bring you great reward, as opposed to staying on the surface. It might feel challenging at first. Many of the participants in expressive writing studies are initially upset by the process, but they ultimately experience it as the valuable and meaningful tool it is.

Creating Positive Emotions

Journaling is not only about releasing yourself from negative emotions. As a counter to these intense emotions, and perhaps some light relief, in this section I will take you through some of the positive emotions journaling can inspire in you. Not only will you get the relief of shedding any trauma and stress through these management techniques, you can also create happiness and other positive emotions for yourself. I have mentioned the two types of positivity gained through journaling in earlier chapters—the positive emotions gained from succeeding at a goal, and advancing your life towards your dream for it, and the enjoyment you can take from the process of journaling. Carving out time for yourself to engage in an enjoyable hobby can also provide you with self-confidence and a sense of fulfillment at the time well spent. It might seem contradictory to explore the science of happiness. We often find that we cannot point to a clear reason for our happiness, or that it is impossible to find an accurate language to describe it. However, there are scientific ways of researching and quantifying happiness that allow us to look in detail at the impact journaling can have on your mood.

One clear method of quantifying happiness is the amount of goals set. Setting positive, future-facing goals is already a good indicator of positive mental health, as it demonstrates your confidence in both yourself and the future. If your goals are realistic and achievable, they also demonstrate the accuracy of your worldview. People struggling with a lack of self-belief or mental health issues are less likely to challenge themselves, as they believe they are incapable of success.

Of course, this quantification of happiness goes hand-in-hand with another (rhyming) numerical measure—the amount of goals met. Meeting your goals shows that you are actively living your life, trying your best to push yourself forward, and demonstrates a positive mental attitude. Every goal met is another improvement in your life, and so naturally your happiness will increase, as you get closer and closer to your ideal life. A research study has shown that journaling is explicitly connected to your sense of optimism, with those that journal showing increased levels of optimism, and therefore happiness (Ackerman, 2019). Optimism will not only push you to create new challenges and goals for yourself to achieve, but also help you overcome any challenges thrown at you. Having a toolkit of resources means you have the self-confidence to meet challenges calmly. Another study has also examined how journaling assists in interpersonal relationships (Ackerman, 2019). You might not think that such a solitary activity as journaling can have an effect on your social interactions, but this study found that those that journaled became friendlier, both more open with their existing friends, and more open to meeting new people and making friends. The confidence gained from journaling allowed people to overcome any fears they had about social interaction, and their increased sense of optimism allowed them to go into these interactions expecting the best, and were therefore rewarded.

Both these studies were specifically looking at gratitude journaling, and while the benefits of gratitude journaling can be broadly mapped onto journaling as a whole, they do stress the importance of reflective journaling. Even if your journal is wholly goal-focused, it can be beneficial to include even a line or two of reflection on your progress towards these, to take full advantage of all the happiness available.

Now that we have looked at the happiness and confidence you can gain as a result of journaling, let's examine the benefits the process of journaling can bring you. Of course, these two are intertwined, and you will feel your enjoyment and confidence grow day by day along your journal writing journey. But there are specific benefits to be gained from the daily act of journaling. Daily journaling allows you to write through stressful events, regulating any difficult emotions brought up, and leaving you resolved and ready to face the new day. It also allows you to identify broader patterns in your life, whether that be difficulties at work, arguments with friends or partners, or unhealthy cycles of thoughts you struggle to break. Keeping a record of your day means that you can see each event in the wider context, identifying patterns between them and keeping track of lessons to implement next time. Writing each day, even when you don't want to, also enhances your creativity. By forcing yourself to write even when you aren't necessarily inspired to do so, you engage the right-hand side of your brain, which is traditionally associated with creative tasks (Bailey, 2018). Fostering connections between your logical brain and your creative brain improves your mental agility, and works the creative muscles you might be neglecting in the rest of your life.

Reducing Negative Emotions

Some of the more obvious impacts journal writing can have on reducing your negative emotions have already been mentioned, either in the discussion about reducing stress specifically, or about increasing positive emotion, which will naturally lessen negative feelings. Gaining control of your life and beginning to implement and achieve goals you believe will reduce any feelings of doubt, inferiority, or stagnation you might be suffering from, and help you look at the world with more optimism, improving your baseline mood. Having established these general impacts that anyone may experience and benefit from when journaling, I want to use this section to look in greater depth at the benefits of journaling for specific mental health issues, that can seriously negatively impact people's moods and behaviour. I will focus on research done into journal writing for those who suffer with depression and anxiety, and examine how it can work to alleviate the burden of these issues. If you suffer from depression or anxiety, I hope this reassures you that journaling has a strong framework that can handle whatever issues you need it to, and that can form part of your treatment plan. If you do not suffer with issues like this, this section can still give you a sense of the depth of work journal writing can do for people.

A wealth of research has gone into the relationship between journaling and mental health issues, starting with its beginnings as a form of therapy. They have looked at a range of high risk population groups, as well as those diagnosed with some form of depressive disorder. These include those dealing with big changes in their lives, such as adolescents or college students, or those who have undergone serious trauma, such as domestic abuse survivors. Journaling has been found to reduce depressive triggers in college students, by channeling worries and excessive thoughts into a secure environment, while treating at-risk adolescents with a program of journal writing was found to be just as effective as traditional cognitive behavioural therapy techniques for alleviating burgeoning symptoms of depression (Ackerman, 2019). This was also the case for a study which explored the benefits of journaling for female domestic abuse survivors (Ackerman, 2019).

Although research has indicated that expressive writing does not necessarily reduce the amount of negative thoughts a person with depression might experience, it softens the impact of these thoughts, leading to an overall reduction in symptoms (Ackerman, 2019). People diagnosed with a depressive disorder, and tested on their "depression scores" found that they reduced significantly once they had completed three days of expressive writing (Ackerman, 2019). Similar reports come from research into the impact of journal writing on anxiety, and in fact journaling is particularly appropriate as part of treatment for problems with anxiety and anxiety disorders. It allows you to identify your automatic thoughts, as well as explore the underlying roots of your anxious thoughts and triggers, which you can then work to challenge. A research study analysing the benefits of journaling for women found that it reduced health problems and anxiety, while another study looking at the impact in educational systems found that journaling assisted students in controlling stress and anxiety, and therefore improved their performance in the classroom (Ackerman, 2019).

Time and Energy

Moving on from the many mental benefits keeping a journal can bring you, in this and the next section I want to turn to an examination of the more practical impacts on your life, looking at first the effect on your available time and energy, and then some more detail on achieving goals. When you start journaling, it might not feel like the most effective use of your time. If you are fired up and ready to start making active progress on your goals, spending your time sedentary, sitting and writing, can feel counterproductive. This can be enhanced by the demands journaling makes on your time—depending on your writing style and type of journal, you could be spending up to an hour a day on this practice. If your schedule already feels too busy, it can feel like journaling is only making your situation worse. However, the initial short term demands of keeping a journal reap long term benefits, repaying the time and energy you put in several times over. You will soon find the small commitment you make to journaling starts to free up your schedule, and create more time for you to focus on what is important to you, whether that is your hobbies, time spent with others, or starting to take action on your goals.

As I have previously mentioned, when you make a daily log of how you spend your time, you can quickly see where time is being wasted, or where you are not using it productively. At a base level, journaling helps with this, as you can start to streamline those areas of wasted time, be it time spent procrastinating, or mindlessly scrolling through FaceBook. However, journaling also teaches you to be creative about your time. This is especially true of time you cannot control, or that is a necessity for your work or domestic life. Can you multitask during your commute, or doing household chores, to work towards your goals? You might listen to a podcast on an informative topic, or practice another skill or language, or read a book by someone in the field you wish to move into. Depending on the flexibility of your workplace, you might be able to maximise your time at work by either changing when you work, or how productive your work hours are.

This will naturally start to impact your energy levels. Having more time to focus on activities you have chosen to do, and spending this time more productively, will make you feel more active. Anything that drains your time also drains your energy. You might find that, similarly to time, there is an adjustment period when you change your schedule, or add in a new activity, where you do feel tired, or busy. This should alleviate once you have completed the 30 day period necessary for all new habits, but if it does not, you might want to reconsider your commitment, and reduce it to a more manageable level for the time being. However, with successful schedule reorganizations, you should feel re-energised by the changes, helped by the mental satisfaction of knowing you are making the best use of your time.

Achieving Goals

The message of this book is informed by my twin careers as personal trainer and counselor, as I have stressed not only the mental benefits of journaling, but the sense of purpose and achievement it can provide you with. Counselling focuses much more on the wellbeing of the mind, whereas being a personal trainer is all about helping people to make concrete changes to their body and their lifestyle, by setting clear goals and working steadily to push their limits. Journaling is a combination of both these approaches, able to help you improve your mind and lifestyle in harmony. But how exactly does it help you make these concrete changes and achieve your goals? It does so by equipping you with three skills necessary to take control of your life. These are the Three A's—the Ability to recognise mistakes, Accountability, and the Acceptance truth.

I will take you through each of these in turn, looking at how each one helps you, but I also want to stress now that these skills work in conjunction with each other. If you have one, such as the ability to recognise your mistakes, but fail to develop the sense of accountability needed to own them and learn from them, you will not progress towards your end goal, and might in fact only damage your self-belief further. So when you think about these skills, think about them in tandem, and try to consciously practice them together. When you recognise a mistake you might have made, take responsibility for it, accept the truth of the situation, and make a plan of action from there.

The first A is "Ability," the ability to recognise mistakes and issues that either you or another person has made. By keeping a record of your day, and anything that makes an impression on you, you have all the context behind an event, and can see it as part of a wider history of actions, instead of as an isolated event. For example, you might have an argument with a friend. You feel like their anger is coming out of nowhere, and react defensively, as you believe you have done nothing wrong. You storm home to journal about it, writing an angry entry about how unfair your friend was being. However, if you take the time to read through your previous entries, you realise that actually you have blown off their invitations to meet up several times, and when you do meet them, you've turned up late. Your friend was not just randomly upset, but was hurt by what they saw as a lack of interest in and respect for their friendship and time. Often we hurt people accidentally, not realising the effects our words and actions are having. Journaling helps you develop that sense of self-awareness and critical distance, to recognise mistakes you have made, and to see how they are affecting your relationships and work performance without you realising. It might take time to get your journaling to this point of awareness, but the more you work on it, the better you'll get.

The second A is "Accountability," taking responsibility for your actions. Even if your actions were an accident, or your intentions were good, it is still important that you own these as actions you have made, and accept the outcome of these. This might sound unpleasant or intimidating, and it can be tough at first, but this is the necessary flipside of taking control—you cannot merely pick and choose which of your actions you have control over, but have to accept that everything you do is an action you choose to take, even if it is a choice made from limited or difficult options. This also means however, that when you take accountability for all of your choices, you also have total control over what you do. This is a freeing prospect—you do not necessarily have to react in the way you feel others want you to, and can make choices based on how they will make you feel, and how they progress you towards your goals.

The third and final A is "Acceptance." Although acceptance is a necessary part of the first two A's, here it encompasses a wider sense of the Acceptance of truth. Journaling gives you the truth of the situation, both in terms of what actually happened, as in the example with the upset friend, and how you feel about it. The sense of privacy and security your journal should provide will make you comfortable enough to share your deepest truths, whether they be your true feelings about your job, a friend you secretly struggle with, or ambitions you are too scared to say out loud. Accepting the truth about uncomfortable situations will give you the knowledge and power to begin to transform them into more comfortable ones. This again is facilitated by journaling's use of both the left and right brain. The left brain is preoccupied with the act of writing, making sure that you get down everything you want to, while the right side of your brain is able to dig deep into your feelings, and subconscious intuition, bringing you closer to the truth.

Physical Benefits

Having looked at the practical impact journaling can have on your life, I now want to look at the impact it can have on your body. Many of my personal training clients were surprised when I asked them to keep a journal—they were used to keeping records of the exercises they had done, the food they had eaten and how their body felt as a result of this, but many of them had not taken this further into the emotional and mental territory of true journaling until I asked. They were surprised to find that doing this kind of journaling, more similar to the style used in my counselling practice, also had a massive impact on how they felt in their body, and did create real, physical change in them. Asides from their confidence, their posture and muscular imbalances also made astounding progress in the right direction.

We must not underestimate the power of the connection between the mind and the body, and although journaling only uses your mind and your writing hand, it has a massive impact on all of you. I will start by going through a few of the physical effects, before looking in more detail at two key ways journaling affects your body, namely the effects of stress reduction, and the improvement it makes to your immune system.

Before getting into the physical impacts everyone might experience, I want to just take a moment to explore some of the considerations people with disabilities or chronic health conditions might have. Because it is less physical, journaling is a feasible activity for many disabled people, especially as it is also less expensive, and requires fewer materials. In fact, a research study into the effects of journaling on those suffering from chronic or continuous medical conditions demonstrated that it does still have significant impact (Smyth, 2018). In the same way I reassured those suffering from mental health conditions that the issues they face are not too extreme to be helped by journaling, I want to reassure those with serious physical conditions. The research study demonstrates this, as it concluded that journaling is an acceptable tool for medical patients, those already experiencing some form of physical illness, to cope with and successfully alleviate symptoms of stress and anxiety caused by their other conditions. Therefore, if you have a medical issue, the following two sections on the physical benefits of journaling are still of use to you, as you will still experience them.

Effects of Reducing Stress and Improving Mood

Stress is not only damaging to our mental health, but also to our bodies, taking a significant toll on all aspects of our body. Starting at the top, it can increase the frequency and intensity of headaches, as well as disrupt your sleeping patterns and even cause insomnia. Stress causes your heart to beat faster, and your blood vessels to restrict, and the high heart rate and blood pressure can affect your arteries, increasing your risk of a heart attack. It also affects your stomach, increasing acid production leading to heartburn, or causing issues in your digestive system. The extra sugar released into your blood during times of stress creates high blood sugar, which can then build over time to leave you more at risk of type 2 diabetes. You might also experience issues with your reproductive systems, whether that's finding it hard to conceive, irregularities in your menstrual cycle, or erectile dysfunction. All of this can combine to make you age prematurely as well. I say this not to scare you, but to impress upon you how serious stress is, and how important it is to manage it.

Journaling, as a successful form of stress management, reduces these risks. It has been proven to lower blood pressure, reducing the strain on your heart, and improve the functioning of your liver, which produces the excess sugar (Baikie and

Wilhelm, 2005). Many of these impacts have a domino effect. If you are less stressed, and therefore sleeping better, you will find that your mental processing capability improves; similarly being less stressed can reduce the impact of digestive issues such as Irritable Bowel Syndrome (IBS), which can in itself be a major cause of anxiety and worry. In some cases, IBS can be an example of a psychosomatic illness, one that has its roots in stress, but expresses itself physically in the body. Not only is this often painful to cope with, but the frustration and confusion over the roots of the illness can be just as damaging. Journaling helps with this by relieving stress, and keeping you firmly in the experience of your body, allowing you to monitor triggers and remedies to give you back control.

Immune System Improvement

Some of the improvements to your immune system as a result of journal writing will be a side effect of the reduced pressure stress places on your body. In a heightened state of stress, your body is dealing with so many internal stressors that it is much easier for an external one, such as a virus, to get past your defenses. As your stress decreases, your immune system will get stronger. However, you can be experiencing no or minimal stress, and still feel the benefits of journaling on your immune system. Keeping a journal strengthens the cells within your system, improving its efficacy and reducing the chances of you getting ill. Researchers have examined various aspects of the immune system, and found that in every case, it improved with journaling (Baikie and Wilhelm, 2005). This broad improvement in strength has also been found to take place in specific illnesses. A clinical trial in 1999 examined the effect of expressive writing on people with asthma or rheumatoid arthritis (Smyth, 1999). Patients journaled about their most traumatic memories for four months, and their physical health and symptoms clinically assessed throughout. The trial found that both asthma and arthritis sufferers who had completed the expressive writing task reported increased physical health, and a reduction in severity of symptoms.

CHAPTER 4

TRICKS OF THE TRADE

In this chapter, we'll continue on from the information given in Chapter Two, but instead of looking at what to say, we'll look at different ways to say it. I'll take you through a different range of techniques you can use to express yourself in your journal. Because I discussed prompt and gratitude journaling in such detail in Chapter Two, I will not mention them here, but please still consider them when you decide what technique to employ in your journal.

Each technique here will come with a description of what it is, how to do it well, and the advantages of using it. Some of the techniques may involve aspects of another style, and once you're comfortable, you can pick and choose between them if needed, to create a consistent method that works for you. You might also find that as situations in your life change, you might want to supplement your daily journal method with another added technique. For example, if you take a short term course that means you are meeting new people, you might want to add in character sketches to your journal, allowing you to capture the new people you are spending this brief amount of time with. If you are going through a difficult patch in a relationship, whether with a romantic partner, friend or family member, writing an unsent letter to them can help you clarify and express your emotions safely. Each of these techniques is an arrow in your quiver, to be used when you need it.

Bullet Journaling

You might already be familiar with bullet journaling, or the name at least. It is a form of journaling that has risen exponentially in popularity over the past few years. Created by Ryder Carroll, it sprung from his issues making notes due to his learning disability, and the desire to create a system that would work for him. Lucky for the rest of us, he has shared his bullet journaling process with us. I will outline the process below, but for more information you can check out his website, https://bulletjournal.com/pages/learn.

HOW TO SET UP THE BULLET JOURNAL

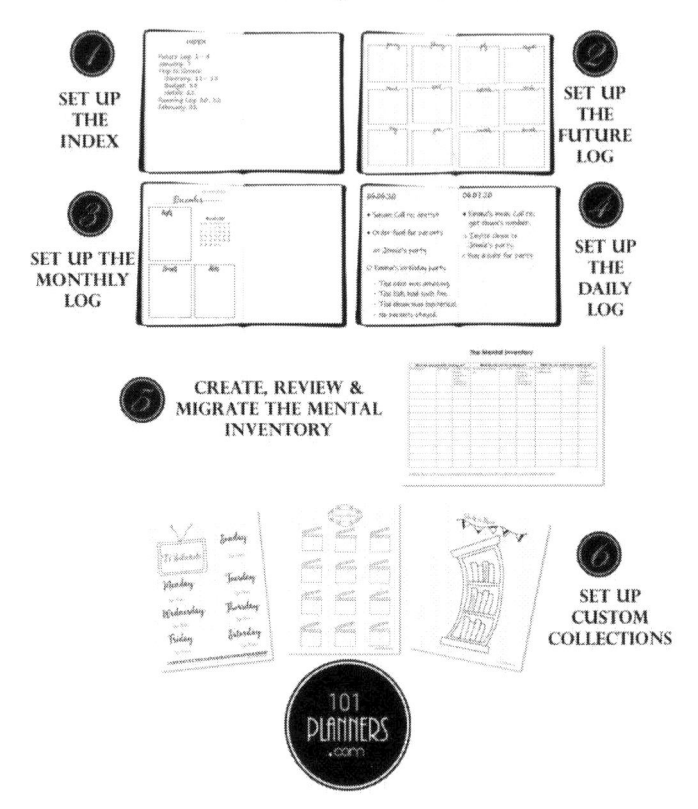

The bullet journal is a framework of modules, called Collections. There are four core Collections essential to the journal, the Index, Future Log, Monthly Log and Daily Log. The Index functions much as any index does, except it lives at the front of your journal. It is important to number the pages of your journal, to make sure you can fully utilise the benefits of the Index, which will allow you to quickly see where your other Collections are. The Future Log is a way of keeping track of dates that will happen after the current month of writing. You might use a year long template, or stick to a six month guide. This is the place to keep track of birthdays, holiday plans and significant deadlines. Looking at your Future Log will give you an overview of the near future, keeping you motivated and excited.

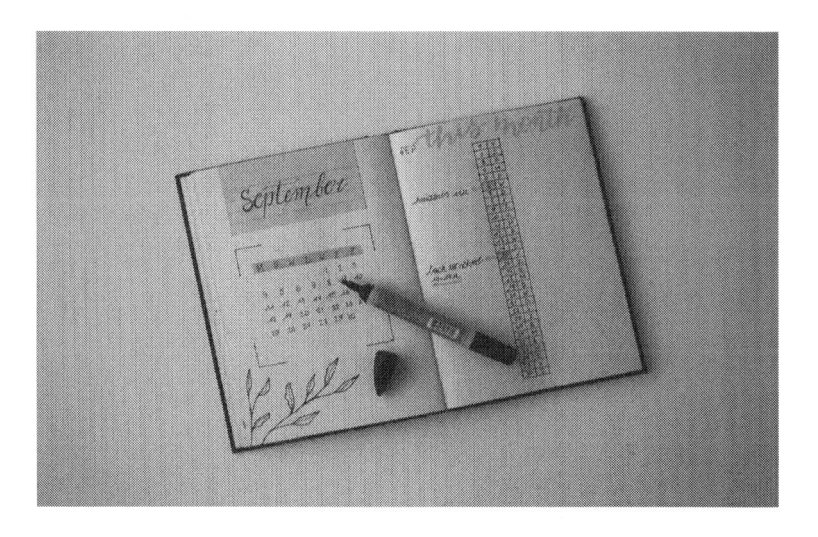

Each month, you can move items in the Future Log for that month to your Monthly Log, as shown above. The Monthly log consists of two pages. One is a Calendar that gives you a quick overview of the month, much like the Future Log. The second page is a Task page, and here you can write down any goals you want to achieve this month. The Daily Log is next, and here you record the events of the day, the tasks you need to complete and whether you do them, and any notes from the day. These are the essential Collections in a bullet journal, but you can add in any others, such as lists, gratitude logs, habit trackers, or even mind maps and doodles.

As the name implies, your logs will traditionally be made up of bullet point entries, using three different symbols to differentiate between Tasks, Notes and Events. For Events, use a circle bullet point, for Notes, a dash, and for Tasks, a solid dot, like the ones I have used for the prompt list. Task bullet points can be further separated into five categories, with the simple dot of an incomplete task transforming into a cross when completed, a forward arrow when moved into a separate week or different collection, a backwards arrow for tasks that have moved into the Future Log, and simply drawing a line through it if the task no longer needs completing. This way, just by looking at the bullet points, you can see what Events, Notes and Tasks you need for your day.

More context can be given to these basic bullet points by adding extra symbols, called Signifiers. One basic Signifier you might want to employ is the asterix, which can be used to signify urgent or important Tasks that absolutely need to be achieved in that time frame, but you can invent your own, depending on what extra information you regularly need about your bullet points.

The movement of bullet points, which I briefly touched on with forwards and backwards arrows, is called Migration. Each month when you make your new Monthly spread, check the old one for incomplete Tasks. Move any you still feel need to be done to your new Monthly spread using a forward arrow, rewriting the task in the new Log, and strike through those you feel aren't important moving forward. Considering your Tasks like this, and making the effort to categorise and move them will help you sift out which ones are actually important and necessary, and which are wasting your time and energy.

Perhaps obviously, bullet journaling is intended to be a way of creating a daily log of your life. One advantage of its Rapid Logging form is that it keeps your life clear and organized, giving you a sense of control. The Migration system is useful for forcing you to consider how you spend your time, and what your priorities actually are. Although its basic structure is as a scheduling tool, it has the flexibility for you to add the deeper thoughts and considerations that make a journal, whether that's a short paragraph in your Daily Log or a longer Collection about a specific issue or goal. You can also take aspects of the journal that resonate with you into a more flexible format, if you find the framework of the journal too restrictive. Many bullet journalers also cite the aesthetic pleasure they get from their journal as a motivating factor, as it can be a rewarding creative task that you will look forward to spending time doing.

Character Sketches

A character sketch is a useful way of immortalising the people around you in your journal. You might want to use this technique to capture a family member or a friend. This can be a really valuable way of seeing that loved one through new eyes, and renewing your love and appreciation for them. Doing this before a celebratory occasion, like their birthday, can refresh your thoughts about them and help you make that day special. On the other hand, if a relationship is going through a difficult patch, doing a character sketch of the person will clarify your feelings, as you'll either realise the ways you two have changed and grown apart, or be able to realise the importance of your relationship, and work to save it. You can also use this to document your friends and family before periods of upheaval. If you are graduating college, or moving cities, making character sketches of your friends before everything changes can be a source of great comfort, and remind you in later reflection what life was like for you then. You do not just have to make character sketches of people you know however. You could document the people you spend a short but intense amount of time with, whether on a cruise or a course, making a sketch at the beginning and end of your time with them, and seeing the changes in your relationship. Character sketches are frequently used as starting points for stories, but here we will use them as a way to create a snapshot of a person.

It can be hard to know where to begin a character sketch. Writing down everything you know about that person can easily get confusing and overwhelming, and instead, you might want to break it down into categories. Write their name at the top of your journal page, and then make space for five different lists around the page. Label these "Appearance," "Actions," "Speech," "Location," and "Feelings."

Under Appearance, write down anything you can about that person's appearance. You can refine your sketch by going beyond basic details like hair and eye color. What is the feature you use to recognise them in a crowd? How does their face change when they are happy, or upset? What is their favourite outfit?

Under Actions, think about any habits this person has, or any routines they stick to. Are they clumsy? Do they have a favourite activity or sport? How do they express their emotions?

For Speech, consider how they talk, as well as what they say. Are they softly spoken? Do they always greet you in the same way? Do you have nicknames for each other, or any inside jokes between you?

Location does not mean where they are at this moment, but where you see them the most or where they enjoy spending most of their time. Here you can describe the scene in more detail.

Finally, for Feelings, think about how they make you feel. If this feels hard to express in words, think about what you look forward to when seeing them, or how you feel after doing so. By organizing your thoughts into these categories, you will be able to build up a picture of this person, which you can supplement with an actual picture if you wish of course!

Character sketches are best done as an addition to a journaling system, rather than forming the backbone of that system. This is because of their narrow focus—they do not provide scope for you to include a daily log, or make plans towards your goals. Instead, think of them as useful extras to your daily routine. As I have mentioned, they can add an emotional snapshot to your journaling, or help you clarify your feelings. With a little creativity, they can be used as part of the goal-setting process. Making a character sketch of someone you need to engage with in order to achieve your goals, such as a difficult boss for example, can help you consider and clarify how you will approach that person, and what strategy will work best in order to get what you need from the interaction.

Clustering/Mind Mapping

Clustering, or mind mapping, is a form of journaling that combines organization with creativity, allowing you to actively see the connections between topics and form more, refining your thought process. Creating a mind map about a topic can be an easier way to see the big picture and the finer details, as opposed to a simple list of notes. Cluster journaling has been proven to improve problem solving ability, enhance concentration and focus levels, and assist memory retention.

It is best to use a mind map for a specific purpose, such as planning a project at work or home, studying a topic, or putting a wider goal in place. This works especially well for things you know have a lot of complex factors, or things that need to be considered. Holding all the information in your head at one time can be confusing, especially if you have to remember the various ways each factor interlocks with others. For example, you might make a mind map entitled "Five Year Plan," with sections dedicated to "Work," "Relationships," "Travel," "Home." These broader sections might connect—if you plan to get married in the next five years, that financial expense might need to be reflected in the "Work" section, a potential honeymoon in the "Travel" section, and your plans for settling into married life might affect your "Home." A mind map like this can give you a broad picture of what you want your life to be like, as well as flag up areas that you want to investigate in further detail.

Practically, I would advise making mind maps in pencil, or any other medium that can easily be erased and changed. Until you start your mind map, you don't have a clear idea of all the connections you will be making, and keeping it flexible means you can change your map as you go, making sure it is clear and legible.

Start with a clear topic in the centre of the page—this can be the name of the topic, or a drawing or symbol that represents it to you. Then draw a series of lines from this central circle outwards, keeping them well spaced apart. These are your spider legs, each representing a different key word relevant to your topic. From here, you can begin to add branches to these, expanding into further detail. In order to keep your clusters clear and useful, keep these tips in mind. Write on the branches, as this will give your map a sense of dynamism, and allow you to see the movements between branches more clearly. Be careful also not to write too much—you want to keep your notes concise, focusing on key words and short sentences at most. Get creative with color, word size and capital letters to provide emphasis and variety to your map. You can also vary the size and thickness of your arrows to provide more information. To keep track of all of these, you might wish to keep a key at the side of the page, or on a separate sheet of paper, that will allow you to understand your thought process when you come to review your map.

Again, cluster journaling is probably not going to be a replacement for a daily journal. It would be possible to do so, using each day as a central topic, and if you find that the format of mind mapping is the clearest way for you to understand information, then of course embrace it. But for most of us, mind mapping is another useful addition to our journaling tool box, to be used where it would bring most benefit. Mind maps can be a valuable starting point, giving you a clear sense of what you know, what you need to find out, and what your next steps should be.

Captured Moments

A captured moment is similar in form and intention to a character sketch, but can be slightly more complex. The principle of a character sketch, wishing to capture the essence of someone important to you or to your life at that moment, is expanded out to any important moment. This can be a milestone achievement you wish to remember, such as a new job offer, or the moment they announce your name at graduation, a practice you engage in regularly, like a birthday, religious festival or cultural event, or simply a way to focus on the details of your day to day life.

Many of us experience major life events slightly in a blur, overwhelmed by the excitement of the day. Picking one moment of the day to focus on can be a valuable counter to this blur, forcing you to reflect on the day and decide what aspects of it made it so magical. Making time to further reflect through journaling about this moment not only improves your memories of the day, but gives you a written record of it to treasure, that will also act as a spark for those memories. This can be especially valuable as part of a repeated ritual. Capturing one moment of your birthday each year will provide key details that will give you a sense of who you were at each age, what circumstances you were living in, what you enjoyed and valued, and who you felt was most important to you. You might enjoy the process of moment capturing so much that you incorporate it into your daily log. Depending on what works for you, you could use it as a space of reflection every day, choosing the moment of that day that is most valuable to you, or you enjoyed the most, or you feel exemplified that day. If this feels like too much, you could make it a weekly event, or pick one day a week to try this added moment of reflection.

When attempting to capture a moment in words, a good way to start is with the practical aspects of the situation. Where were you? Who were you with? What time of day was it? What had happened in the build up to the moment? What were you discussing? Move into the more emotional aspects of it—how were you feeling? Were you tired, or preoccupied with earlier events? Was this an activity you expected to enjoy, or one you thought you would hate? If needed, you can use some of the questions raised in the Character Sketch section if the moment relies heavily on who you were interacting with.

Now that you have set the scene, describe the moment. You might want to again start with the literal facts of the event, before moving into your thoughts and feelings at the time. Then, spend some time reflecting on the moment—how did it make you feel for the rest of the day? Why did you choose this moment to record? What about this moment could you learn from, and try to replicate again? Adding in these moments to your journal can make it feel more connected to your life, and help you move away from a bare boned diary entry.

Time Capsule

Creating a time capsule in your journal follows the same principles as capturing moments. You want to paint a picture of the scene, so when you return to it you feel as though you are transported back there. A time capsule differs from capturing a moment in that the time capsule is often much broader, encompassing more of your life than a single moment. If you can choose a single moment to capture the whole of your life at that time, then go for it, but many of us will struggle to choose just one. Your journal is by nature future facing, but writing a time capsule is directly writing with the future in mind—think about what future you would want to know about your life now, and try to capture those things.

If getting your life onto paper feels like too big a task, you can use the capturing moment technique if you feel that is a helpful way to start writing, by choosing a moment or two from each area of your life, such as college, work, family, or your hobbies. These moments will build up and coalesce into a bigger collage of your life at this moment, that you will be able to look back on later. As I also mentioned in the Captured Moments section, you can tie your time capsule to a certain event, such as a birthday or holiday, and use these annual celebrations as a time of reflection as well.

If you want to make sure your time capsule is comprehensive, you can use brief notes and bullet points to cover the facts of each area of your life, and then move to longer writing about how you feel about these things, and what you enjoy. However, so long as a time capsule includes all the aspects of your life that are most important to you, don't feel any pressure to cover your life in exhaustive detail. Make sure as well to include a few fun details—what are your favourite songs, or books right now? What item of clothing are you wearing on repeat? What snack are you craving? What do you have for lunch most regularly? As an addition to your regular journal practice, a time capsule can be a wonderful way to think seriously about your life now, as well as think about where you might be when you read it in the future.

Unsent Letters

There are two types of unsent letters you can write: ones addressed to yourself and ones addressed to others. Let's start with ones you write to yourself. Writing a letter to your future self can be another way of making a time capsule, telling yourself what is important to you right now, and what you hope your life will be like when you're reading it.

You don't just have to write to your future self, however; you can write to your younger self as well. This can be an amazing tool to see how far you have come, and reflect on the events you've experienced and the challenges you've overcome. You could write one to your past self as part of a reflection after every goal you achieve, congratulating yourself on your success and reflecting on what strategies worked the best for you.

Writing a letter to a younger self can also be soothing, especially if you've experienced something traumatic in the past. Talking to your younger self and reassuring them can also work to reassure yourself now, and remind yourself of how far you've come, and what you had to endure. If you find it difficult to compliment yourself, try writing the letter from someone else's perspective, either someone supportive you know, or a stranger. Writing from their perspective might help you open up, and be able to recognise your achievements and positive attributes. This type of letter writing can be intensely emotional, and might bring up some uncomfortable feelings from the past. By warning you of this now, I hope that it will prepare you for any difficult feelings, and you can make sure you're in a comfortable headspace to begin this process.

The second type of unsent letter is one written to someone else. There are several reasons you might want to write a letter to someone and not send it. One key reason is that it can be a healthy way to release anger and frustration, especially in a situation that cannot be resolved by a healthy discussion with the source of your anger. So this might include a bad boss, who repeatedly saddles you with extra work, or never gives you credit for your work or ideas, but that you cannot raise these issues with for fear of being fired. Writing an angry letter can provide you with an outlet, reducing your pent up stress about the situation, with all the benefits we learnt about in Chapter three.

Writing these letters can be a productive tool in your toolkit to deal with grief, if you are unlucky enough to be experiencing that right now. It can be a wonderful way to continue the relationship you had with that person, and still feel that sense of closeness to them.

An unsent letter can be a wonderful way to express your feelings of love, whether for those you can no longer tell, or those you do not want to. You might not want to confess your feelings to someone, or know for sure they will not be reciprocated, but expressing them in a letter can give you a sense of closure.

All these forms of letter writing in fact, can give you closure, clarity, and a sense of calmness. You might recognise a need to write an unsent letter if something repeatedly comes up in your regular journaling practice, and you feel as though a letter will give you the catharsis necessary to move on.

Dialogues

Writing a dialogue might feel like something only playwrights do, but if it works for you, it can be a productive journaling tool. Take a situation you are nervous about, or need to be prepared for, and write out what you want to say. This can be a really useful way to clarify your ideas into speech, and make sure that all the information you want to convey is being conveyed clearly and confidently. A dialogue then goes one step further, as you can then consider what responses you might get to your speech, and prepare responses to them. In order to keep this a productive exercise, you need to try and be as realistic about other people's potential responses as possible. This can be hard, but will ultimately make you better prepared for the actual situation.

Creating a dialogue can be a useful way of practicing for professional situations and personal ones. You might need to have a difficult conversation with a friend, family member or partner, and workshopping potential ways the conversation will go will make you feel more confident, as well as reducing the chances of the conversation being derailed, or you saying something you later regret. You might also have a presentation or an interview approaching, and journaling potential dialogue could prepare you and ease your nerves.

Although I cautioned you to keep these dialogues realistic, writing an idealistic or wildly unrealistic dialogue has a different, but still useful, purpose. You might feel silly, or childish, doing it, but writing out the dialogue to a dream conversation can still boost your mood, as well as help you get a clearer sense of what your dreams and goals look like. For example, writing out the dialogue between you and your crush, in which they declare their undying love for you, and list the endless reasons why you are the best person in the world, might feel like a pointless teenage activity, but does serve a range of purposes. Firstly, your journal is a private place for you to have fun in, and embrace all of your emotions; secondly, thinking of what your crush would say can be an excellent confidence building exercise; and thirdly, it might help you clarify what exactly you are looking for in a romantic partner, or solidify your desire for one, which you can then take action on.

Lists

For many people, lists will form the backbone of their journaling practice, so it is important to work out a method of list making that works best for you. They can be an excellent way of organizing all the information you keep in your journal, from the daily tasks you need to complete to important events to the steps you will take to meet your goals. The Bullet Journaling section outlined one method of keeping your lists organized and clear, but if you find that system isn't right for you, there are some simple rules to keep in mind when making a list. Think about the amount of information you need for each point—will seeing something like "meeting 4.30 p.m." spark your mind to remember the rest of the details? Or do you need to include who it's with and what it's about in your list?

With this information in mind, think about how much space you will need for your list. Make sure everything is nicely spaced out on your page, as that means you will be able to see the key points at a glance. If you are worried about how to complete a task, make a list of the sub tasks within it, and work your way through those instead. Make sure if you don't keep your list visible throughout the day that you then return to it frequently, ticking off your accomplishments and reminding yourself what you still need to do.

Lists can also be more creative. You can make lists about anything—keep a running list of favourite songs, or films, or books you've read. You can use lists to be reflective, counting up your favourite experiences of the year, or your favourite things about yourself. Lists can be future-facing, holding space for all your dreams and goals. You can also use lists to try and solve problems, using a quota. With this method, write your problem at the top of the page, and then set a quota of solutions to come up with. Try and make this a totally exaggerated number, like 100. Having to think of 100 solutions to your problem might seem crazy, but it will force you to consider all the possible options, and think outside of the box of typical solutions. The combination of practicality, flexibility and creativity inherent in a list makes it an incredibly valuable journal writing method.

Worst Case Scenario

Although it might be unpleasant to consider the worst case scenario option, it can help you in the long run, either to work to avoid it ever happening, or to ensure that if it does, you will be well equipped to deal with it. You do not have to consider large scale worst case scenarios, like apocalypse or natural disasters. Dwelling too much on unrealistic worst case scenarios can have the opposite effect, making you paranoid instead of calm, and panicked instead of cool and collected.

To practice this, take one of the sources of worry that is most pressing at this moment as your focus instead. This could be public speaking you have to do, a difficult project or assignment, or an interview you really want to go well. Write the situation at the top of the page, keeping it brief. You will go into more detail when you start the worst case process, so try not to get bogged down in details in the introduction.

Once you have begun to think about the situation, write down the worst thing that could happen. This can often be quite quick and instinctual, as it is often the worst case scenario that has been at the forefront of your mind, causing you to worry. Try and dig down into the scenario, no matter how uncomfortable you find it.

Once you have the unpleasant details, you can then start a new section. What are the possible reactions you could have to this scenario actually happening? Acknowledge how upset you would be, but also try to think of practical steps you could take to alleviate it. Working through the worst case and out the other side into a range of solutions should hopefully calm your fears about it, and reassure yourself that no matter what happens, you and your journal can cope with it all. It can also be valuable to return to the worst case scenario after you've accomplished the task, incorporating it into your reflection and expressing your gratitude that you were able to cope.

Goal Setting

I have discussed goal setting as a keystone of journaling throughout this book, but here I want to focus on concrete ways to use your journal to clearly set out your goals, and work to achieve them. How you do this will depend on how your mind works, and what knowledge you already have about your goal. If you do not have a clear idea of your goal, but know that you want to make a change in your life, go through your daily journal entries and make a note of any issues that come up repeatedly—maybe frustrations at work, or issues in a relationship. As an example, let's say that you are chronically late for everything, despite trying to be on time, and it is starting to frustrate your friends and colleagues.

Once you have identified your problem, brainstorm possible solutions. If you're frustrated at work, is this because you have outgrown your role and need more of a challenge, or a move sideways into a different position, or is it a smaller issue, like a difficult project, at an otherwise enjoyable job? In my example, the solution is simple—you need to improve your time management. Then think of ways you can achieve this solution. There might only be one major option, such as moving jobs, or a range of different size accommodations you can make, such as taking on more work that interests you and talking to your boss and improving your work and life balance.

Once you have decided what you are going to do, make a list of all the steps you have to take to achieve your goal, breaking tasks down if needed. Then start to schedule the changes you will make. In the example, this might sound like this: "To improve my time keeping, I will wake up half an hour earlier to give myself enough time in the morning. I will start this tomorrow, and I will continue it for the 30 days needed to form a habit. If I cope well with this, I will add in another habit, setting alarms for when I need to leave the house to meet people, and do that for 30 days. Then I will review whether my lateness has been solved." Working steadily and calmly on your habits and goals means that you are less likely to be intimidated by challenges, and much more likely to rise to meet them.

Stream of Consciousness

A stream of consciousness, or free writing, is a technique where you simply pick up your pen and write down whatever thoughts are in your head at that moment, without trying to make sense of them or structure them. If you have nothing to say, simply write that over and over until you have another thought, even if it is simply that writing one sentence over and over is getting boring!

You might be wondering how this technique can help you take control of your life, as it might sound directionless and unfocused. However, it is intensely focused on your thought processes, and as you spend more time paying attention to this, you'll increase your knowledge about yourself, which you can then use to set your goals. Some people also find it intensely beneficial as a way to clear their minds, as all the worries that have been churning through your mind are now caught on paper, helping you get a sense of perspective on them and begin to formulate solutions.

It can also be an intensely productive exercise. Forcing yourself to write can stretch your mind, and you can come up with useful new ideas, or solutions you wouldn't have previously considered. This is helped by the fact that stream of consciousness writing is very freeing—writing your thoughts means you don't have time to consider whether your grammar is correct, or whether your sentence makes sense. You do not have to be polite, or worry about punctuation. This is solely about you and your thoughts. We censor ourselves in many ways in our daily life, and this is an opportunity to be as honest with yourself as you'd like to be, so try not to hide behind vague detail, or worry about representing people nicely.

Free writing can be a useful technique to start your day with, clearing your mind of any unfinished business from the day before, and starting fresh and focused again. However, any time you feel like you need to connect with yourself, whether just to check in, or to solve a specific problem, is a good time for a stream of consciousness journal entry. As they are so unstructured, I do recommend you use them as an addition to a structured schedule of entries to tether you.

Dream Journaling

Like stream of consciousness writing, dream journaling can be a valuable way to step out of the ordered conscious mind, and tap into what your unconscious mind is trying to tell you. Most people have a sense of the effect your waking life can have on your dreams, most commonly in cases of stress or high pressure. These emotions can have a negative effect on your sleep as well as your mood, causing disrupted sleep, insomnia, and even nightmares. But you might also find that your dreams can have a reciprocal effect on you. This is not just in terms of how your mood is affected by lack of sleep, but also the effect the content of your dreams can have on you. If you have a positive dream, in which you are happy and successful, you will wake up feeling subconsciously happier and more self-confident. If you have a nightmare, you might wake up feeling on edge or nervous, and this can follow you into the rest of your day. So, if dreams have such an effect on us, how can we record and work with them? Because dreams can easily slip away from us, it is best to record them immediately after waking. Keep your journal close to your bed, to prompt you to record anything you experienced during the night. Write down anything you can remember, even if they're just fragments of dreams.

Of course, if you find you don't dream very often, either this technique might not work best for you, or you might find you only need to record your dreams very infrequently. If you dream regularly, you might consider getting a specific journal for your dreams. Although the science behind dream meanings and symbols is now more disputed, your dreams can still tell you a lot about your life. Any repeated patterns you notice will signify issues significant for your subconscious, and that you should focus on. Try to also get a sense of the mood of the dream, which might tell you more about your own.

Non-Dominant Hand

Although writing with your non-dominant hand might feel like a fun party trick, it can be another valuable way of accessing your inner creativity. At the most basic level, because writing with your non-dominant hand is so foreign to us, it makes the whole project of writing new. We are then less likely to revert to our usual patterns of thought, as we have to pay so much more attention to the movement of our hand. Because it is harder to write, you have to be much more intentional about what you want to say, and you might find that you are able to pare ideas down to their essential qualities. Writing with your non-dominant hand can also open up different areas of your brain, helping you combine creativity and expressivity with logic and rationality (Purcell, 2016.) This strategy does require patience, and again might not work as part of a daily journaling practice (unless you enjoy chaos-like scribbles!), but can be a useful activity if you feel stuck or frustrated, as it will help you shake up your mindset.

CHAPTER 5

PERSONAL DEVELOPMENT

In this final chapter, I want to combine all the information I have given you about the benefits of journaling with the techniques laid out in Chapter Four, to focus on exactly how you can make journaling work for you. Although the benefits of journaling are universal, here I will look at how it can help with specific goals and mental health issues, and you might find that if you do not suffer with these issues, those sections might be less relevant to you. I encourage you to read them if you want, as even if you do not suffer with extreme issues such as anxiety or depression, you might still find tips on how to regulate and boost your mood.

I will begin by briefly looking at the long history journaling has with therapy and counselling practices. Journaling cannot always be used as a substitute for therapy, and if you feel like you need professional help I strongly encourage you to reach out to someone, but it can work perfectly in tandem with it, as I will explore.

The second section of this chapter will function almost as a set of training plans, as I will take you through a number of common issues, and set out ways you can make your journaling intentional, and focus on solving each issue. This epitomizes the lessons I have learnt from each of my careers, and what sets my journaling advice and practice apart from others. While of course, keep in mind that journaling is intensely personal, and that the success of each technique will differ depending on how your brain responds to it, these personal training plans should function as a jumping off point. Once you get started, you will gain a sense of what works for you and what doesn't, and can adjust the plans to work for you.

Relationship With Therapy

Journaling, as you might have guessed, has an incredibly complementary relationship with therapy. They have been intertwined since the 1960s, with Dr. Progoff's Intensive Journal classes, and the subsequent publishing of several books intended to guide the reader to a happier, balanced self, through a combination of journal-based and therapeutic techniques. Frequently, for less impactful issues with mental health, doctors will recommend journaling as a way of learning about and processing your emotions. In more high risk cases, journaling will often be part of a range of strategies used to improve mental health, and alleviate the burden of issues like depression and anxiety. I give all my counselling patients a journal, no matter their issue, as I fervently believe that journaling can not only alleviate problems, but also act preemptively, keeping you emotionally balanced and preventing any recurrence.

Similarities Between Journaling and Therapy

The aim of therapy, especially Cognitive Behavioural Therapy and other talking-based methods, is to get the patient to recognise harmful thoughts, and to create new patterns of thoughts and actions, to move away from damaging thought cycles towards a healthier way of life. To do this, a combination of work with a therapist and homework is used. You might talk through your fears with a therapist, and they can provide a secure dissenting voice for your thought patterns, gently pushing you to question your assumptions and unhealthy beliefs. Often this gentle pushback, or being asked to explain your thoughts further, can prompt you to start to unpick them, and see the unhealthy beliefs at the root of these.

Therapists frequently ask their clients to work on this outside of their often short sessions, as it is only with repetition that you can practice unpacking unhealthy thoughts and replacing them with healthier ones. There are a range of aides to help you with these, and they often come in the form of worksheets. These sheets take you step by step through the process, guiding you. Most obviously, these worksheets echo the process of journaling. By forcing you to write about your thoughts, and consider them more carefully, in both cases you can get a healthier sense of what thoughts are helpful and which are not useful. Just as a prompt would in a journal, the worksheets push you to consider issues you had not previously, and re-examine your thoughts. This is the broader project of both counselling and journaling—to encourage you to become more intimate with your own thoughts, and therefore more in control of them, and your life.

How Journaling can Complement Therapy

Due to the similarities between journaling and therapy, you might believe that there is no need to do both, and that this is an either-or situation. This is not true. If you are seeing a counselor, you absolutely still can keep a journal, and in fact this can be very beneficial for the counselling process.

A quick note of caution here—please do not try and manage serious mental health issues on your own. If you feel like you are endangering yourself, talk to someone you trust, or a professional, who can make sure that your journaling practice is supporting you in the best way, or supplement it with other approaches.

Journaling is a brilliant tool in your tool kit because it enhances your self-awareness. The more self-aware you are, the easier you might find it to identify unhealthy thoughts. Your journal will provide you with a safe space to analyse your thoughts, what you are learning in counselling, and how to apply these lessons to anxiety-provoking events. You can plan to push yourself forward gently and safely, making goals that help you reprogram your thoughts. Journaling is so in tune with the needs and methods of counselling that there is even an explicit "journal therapy" practice, begun and refined by the psychotherapist Kathleen Adams, in which the journal is an essential part of the therapy session, making use of different writing exercises (Adams, n.d.).

Journaling With a Purpose

Although all forms of journaling are done with purpose, whether that is to get a fuller sense of your thought process, to gain control of your life, or to work towards achieving your dreams through the setting of goals, in this section we will look at aiming your journaling practice towards certain issues you might be experiencing. Some of these are more aligned with the idea of journaling as a tool for mental health, as I will look at ways to alleviate negative emotions, control anxiety and cope with trauma. I will also look at ways to positively impact your confidence and self-esteem, as well as more practical considerations such as organizing your life, achieving your goals and managing stressful situations. As I mentioned previously, these training plans are intended as suggestions to get you started, and as you go, if you find that you need to adjust the plan, or replace one technique with another better suited to you, go ahead. This can even be a sign of success, signalling just how well you now know yourself, and your needs. Again, feel free to flick between the plans to find ones that are relevant to you, or contain useful information for you, even if you are not specifically affected by these issues.

Managing Emotions

If your regular journaling practice is bringing up a lot of negative emotions, or signalling your lack of control over these emotions, you might want to supplement your practice with some techniques specifically designed for helping you manage these overwhelming emotions. One technique is the unsent letter, which I mentioned in Chapter Four, and which is especially useful if your emotions are being particularly triggered by another person. Writing a letter to that person can help you express your extreme emotion, and regulate your feelings about them. This is part of a wider strategy called Depth Journaling, in which you explicitly write about the sources of your negative emotions and anxiety, in order to write through them and heal from them. This can use the stream of consciousness technique from Chapter four, as you might find you need to start with surface annoyances before you can move further into your subconscious fears and worries.

Depth journaling can work as a form of cleansing, done daily for a length of time, to purge yourself of past issues and make yourself feel more balanced. Set an intention to sit down every day, perhaps as part of your current journaling routine, and write about one thing that causes negative emotion in you. You might want to set a time limit, if you feel like that could be beneficial for you, and there are prompts available to spark you, such as "What feelings do you avoid?" or "Do you feel validated? If not, why not?" or "What have you taken the blame for in your life?"

If you feel like you need more structure beyond this, there are a couple of exercises you can incorporate into your journaling. The first one helps you to identify your emotions by asking you to describe them in new ways. You can either take the emotion you are feeling currently, or pick one like "happiness" or "embarrassment" to analyze, and ask yourself the question "What color would this feeling be?" You can replace color with another object or concept, such as "music" or "weather." Thinking about emotion like this can challenge your brain to focus on the specific qualities of each one, helping you to identify them in the future.

The second exercise focuses on enhancing your positive emotions. Write a description of a happy time in your life, making sure to get down each detail using the Captured Moment techniques. When you feel sad, return to this description to remind yourself that you have felt happy before and will again.

Increasing Self-Esteem and Self-Love

There are a number of similar exercises you can do to increase your self-esteem. It can be hard to recognise when we have low esteem—we tell ourselves that we are just being realistic, and that it's important to have a clear idea of our strengths and weaknesses. This is true, but if you can name far more weaknesses than strengths, or struggle to think of any achievements you've made, you might want to consider that your sense of yourself is inaccurate, and could do with a boost. Self-esteem, like other thought patterns, can be seen as a muscle—you need to train it in order to get stronger, and then it will become second nature.

One way to boost your self-esteem is to set aside some of your journaling time to focus on this training. Try and make a list of things you like about yourself—these can be anything, but try to focus on aspects of your personality as well as physical things. If this is difficult, start by making a list of compliments other people have given you to give you some suggestions. You can continue this list, by making a note of compliments you receive, but be careful not to focus too much on the validation of others. Other people appreciating you might give you a foundation for your self-esteem, but you need to focus on appreciating yourself, without solely relying on others. Using a prompt is another way to make starting your self-love journey easier—ask yourself questions like:

- What can I forgive myself for?

- What makes me feel my best?

- What makes me feel loved? How can I do this for myself?

- What are the achievements I am most proud of?

- What difficult situations have I survived? What strength has that given me?

- What activities bring me happiness? How can I do more of those?

If you struggle to answer these, do not be discouraged, but keep trying. If you can't come up with ways that you feel your best, try testing a few throughout the week, and come back and see which of them you can add to your list. You can incorporate this training into your daily practice as well. Try to end your journal entries with a list of three things that you either like about yourself, or that you have done well that day.

Increasing Confidence

Self-esteem and self-confidence are intertwined, and so you might want to combine activities from this section with activities in the previous one, for a double-pronged approach. For example, writing about your past achievements will boost your confidence as well. There are exercises you can do to specifically target your sense of confidence to further improve it. One such exercise is to split your journal page in two. On one side, describe a situation where you felt confident and in control. On the other, write about a situation where you didn't feel confident. Then try to examine the difference between these situations—can you identify any factors that contributed to your sense of confidence that you can replicate going forward?

Another exercise you can try is taking time to write about who you want to be. In the ideal version of yourself, what are you doing? What personality traits have you nurtured? It might encourage you to see the seeds of your ideal self in your current one, and the steps you have already taken, as well as solidify your future plans. It will also remind you of the reasons you are trying to build your self-confidence—to ensure you can make this ideal version of yourself a reality. In a similar vein, try writing yourself a pep talk, for when you aren't feeling confident. For the best results, do this as part of your reflective journaling after achieving one of your goals. Having a record of how good you felt achieving your goal will remind you to keep pushing towards your next one.

Affirmations

Affirmations can be a really valuable tool to build up your self confidence, although they can be used to help with any aspect of your mental health you want to focus on. An affirmation is a short statement you can repeat to yourself, that sets a positive intention for your day. You might be sceptical about the power of affirmations to change our mindsets. But throughout this book, I have emphasised the power of writing to change your thoughts, and affirmations are another example of this. Cognitive Behavioural Therapy works on the principle that what you think and do affects your mood and behaviour, and so by changing the negative thought loops you might be stuck in, you transform your mood and then your life. This process takes advantage of your brain's neuroplasticity to do this rewiring.

Setting affirmations is best done in the morning, although you could also set them in the evening for the next day, if that works best with your regular journaling schedule. To give you a sense of what an affirmation is, here are a few examples:

- I am strong and successful.
- I will say no when I need to.
- I am valuable and confident.
- I see success in my future.
- I am calm and in control.
- I am able to cope with whatever happens today.

You are welcome to use any of these examples as your affirmation, and if you need more, there are digital apps you can download that will give you personalised affirmations on your phone for whenever you need them. Some examples include *Unique Daily Affirmations* on the Apple App store, or *I am—Daily Affirmations* if you have an Android device.

It can also be very rewarding to make your own affirmation, that is tailored exactly to you. Use the first person and the present tense in your affirmation, and remember to keep it short and simple. Decide what area of your life you want to focus on. You can set intentions to release yourself from negative beliefs, or encourage your positive qualities. You can also set an affirmation for your day ahead, honing in on specific events that will take place, and the qualities you will need to succeed in them. If you need to, you can set more than one affirmation, but make sure they are simple statements, and don't give yourself too many to focus on at one time. Once you have your affirmations, write them with passion, and repeat the process several times, to properly set the intention in your mind.

Coping With Trauma

Journaling can be a valuable way to cope with trauma and subsequent PTSD, as it better prepares you to manage your symptoms. On a basic level, getting in touch with your emotions and thoughts through your daily journaling will help you feel more in control of your brain, and hopefully reduce symptoms. There are strategies you can utilise to help as well. The first one is documentation. We don't typically write much in present tense in our journals outside of affirmations and free writing, focusing instead on the past events that have happened to us, and our hopes for the future. Documentation is a form of free writing that focuses on how you are feeling in the present. You can do this as many times a day as you need to, and just take five minutes to journal about how you are feeling at that moment. You can focus on physical sensation as well—are you hungry? What can your body feel at that moment? Are you cold or hot?

This technique is designed to help with dissociation, as it returns you to your body, and makes you focus on the present moment. You can do this for a longer period of time, still focusing on your feelings and needs in the present, and it will help you to focus on where you are now, and not your time of trauma.

One method of looking back healthily at your past trauma is containment journaling. It is similar to worst case scenario journaling, as you describe the traumatic moment or anxieties that are burdening you. This can be a delicate process, and you should set a time limit for yourself, and treat yourself to some self-care after. If done properly, it can be a useful way of distancing yourself from the trauma, and containing it within the page. You might want to do this in tandem with a more positive exercise, like a "Love Response" (Amy, 2016). Here, once you have done a section of free writing, you examine it for any issues that have been brought up, and then write a response to those, focusing on giving only support and love.

This might feel silly, but imagine that you are writing to a friend, and show yourself the same love you would show them. In the same vein, you can also use gratitude journaling to reorientate yourself in your life, and focus on the positive.

Stress Management

Stress is an umbrella term that covers a variety of different sensations and triggers. As such, you might find that tips in the Soothing Anxiety section, or Managing Emotions, are also helpful here, and vice versa. However I do have some specific advice for directly targeting stressful situations, and working to handle them successfully. One method is to start by identifying exactly how you are feeling, and what is causing it. This can be done simply by writing "I am feeling . . ." and then finishing it with your emotions. You might start with the blanket "stressed," but try to dig down if you can into more specific adjectives.

Once you have this list, create a list below of the triggers for your feelings. Keep each bullet point short and sweet, so you can clearly see what is causing you to feel overwhelmed. Many of these might be tasks you need to get done—create a list of everything you need to do, and then order everything by priority, considering time sensitivity and overall importance. Once you have this, you can start to insert the tasks into your daily schedule. Hopefully, once you have your tasks planned out, your stress will reduce, as you are back in control. Make sure to schedule in some self-care activities as well to take care of yourself.

Another method of managing your stress is to look closely at your coping strategies—how do you handle stress? Do these strategies work? How could you improve them to take the pressure off yourself? These are longer term methods to alleviate your stress, but I will also give you a couple of quick prompts to use in the moment, to help you ground yourself. These can also be useful for dealing with anxiety if needed. The first one is to take stock of your body. Make a written inventory of how your body feels, and see if there is anything you can then alleviate. This might be tension in your neck or shoulders, tightness in your chest, or clenching your jaw. Try and relax your muscles and take a couple of deep breaths. The other prompt is to imagine a soothing place for you to go and relax, and write about it. Try and describe what you would see, smell, hear and feel when you are there. Writing about this place will help you access it, and relieve your stress.

Improving Organization

Many of the techniques for improving your organizational skills have already been discussed. In the previous section on Managing Stress, I touched on how to prioritise the tasks you need to do, and begin to schedule them into your diary. The Bullet Journaling technique described in Chapter Four is also a useful model for improving your organization. Even if you do not follow all the symbols and logs exactly, the concept of keeping track of tasks in monthly, weekly and daily blocks, with plenty of flexibility between the three, is a useful model to follow to keep track of your wider life.

Starting to organize your life in your journal is the hardest part, as once you have a basic model, you can repeat this with any necessary changes from week to week. It can be useful to start with a broad list of your week, making notes of any regular events, or tasks you have to do every week. Then make a list of any items you would like to, or have to, do each day—these can include your journaling time, your hobbies, time spent with friends, family or pets, or exercise routines.

Start to combine the two, slotting your desired daily activities around your required ones. You might not achieve all of your desired activities in a day, and if you find yourself rushing between them you might need to edit your schedule, but having them in your schedule might prompt you to make time for them, instead of losing time to pointless tasks or procrastination. Looking at your schedule, you might then be able to notice any free sections of time, where you can build in more tasks.

Make sure you are realistic about how long tasks actually take, and what you can achieve, so you don't push yourself beyond your limits and burn out. Adding stuff gradually can be a brilliant way to gently expand your capabilities, and get more done.

Increasing Happiness

This training plan to introduce more joy into your life has four main points, but you will find that the sense of control and success journaling brings you will also naturally increase your levels of happiness. The first strategy to increase your happiness is to take pleasure in the process of journaling. Although it has a serious impact on your life, you should still be able to enjoy it. This is easiest once you have found the journaling method that works best for you, as sitting down to journal can easily be something you look forward to.

Despite the aesthetic image of perfection journaling is associated with, try to let go of any perfectionist tendencies when writing your journal. It is more important that it works for you than to look beautiful. Of course, if you do enjoy the aesthetic aspect of your journal, embrace your artistic side and creativity. To help you enjoy the process, try saying or thinking positive thoughts while doing it. You might feel a little silly thinking "I'm really enjoying doing this," or "I'm so glad I take the time to do this for myself," but as we have seen throughout, your thoughts have incredible power, and you can train your brain into more positive thought patterns. You can also do this after you journal, either by saying "I really loved writing today," or getting more specific. Thinking of something you have immediately gained from that day's journaling will help you see all the benefits it brings to your life, and make you more determined to keep going.

This is a more targeted version of gratitude journaling, which is the second strategy you can use to boost your serotonin levels. I briefly mentioned gratitude journals in Chapter Two, as they can be an excellent prompt to help you begin your journaling journey, but they can also work long term as part of your happiness strategy. Making a conscious choice to be grateful for things in your life not only makes you happier, but more open to the possibilities of happiness around you. You can do this by using a prompt, where you fill in a list of things you are grateful for each day, or just by making a conscious effort to focus on the positive events of your day. If you find you struggle to come up with more than one or two, swapping to a prompt for three or five gratitude items can help you practice. Once you start training your gratitude muscles, you will find it easier and easier to spot positive things in your life, even if they are deceptive at first. Don't just stop at gratitude for others however, but also try to direct this gratitude towards yourself. Thank yourself at the end of your journaling session for taking the time to journal, and for opening yourself up to happiness.

The third method for improving your happiness through journaling is to take advantage of the self-awareness journaling gives you. You will be able to pinpoint moments of true happiness, assess their causes, and work on adding in more of these to your everyday life. Even knowing what makes you miserable can alleviate your misery, because you won't be surprised by it, and can plan mood boosting activities around the negative activity.

The fourth and final tip to increase your happiness is to focus less on lists and activities. Instead of making a to-do list focused on activities, focus on who you will see. This has two aspects—firstly, instead of seeing "coffee" or "lunch" in your schedule and getting stressed, seeing "Eric for lunch" and "Lauren for coffee" can boost your mood, as it focuses your attention on your friends, and on that sense of connection, instead of making each event feel like another boring task to check off. You can also take a connection-first approach to planning your time—make a list of people you want to see, and be intentional about scheduling time with them, to boost your mood. You can then look through your journal and see all the moments of connection you have, increasing your happiness.

Soothing Anxiety

Whether you struggle with a generalised anxiety disorder, or simply want to target any anxious thoughts you might have, the advice here will hopefully help you target your anxieties. You can of course incorporate tips from other relevant sections to create a full toolkit of approaches if you want to. I want to start by briefly mentioning the techniques in Chapter Four that would be especially useful for managing anxiety. Journaling about the worst case scenario can be a good way to lean into your anxiety, acknowledge its fears, and resolve them. If your anxiety is caused by other people, an unsent letter can again work to help you let go of some of the weight you are carrying. On a more foundational level, the control you will have over your life through daily journaling and scheduling should relieve some of your anxieties. To help with this, you can incorporate a miscellaneous note page into your journaling.

Often anxiety can come from trying to hold too much in our heads at one time—even if they are positive things! Keeping a miscellaneous or "everything" notes section means anything you want to remember you can quickly make a note of, and transfer into the appropriate section of your journal at a later date if needed (Thompson, 2017). Instead of having to juggle all these thoughts and ideas in your head, you can rest reassured that your journal has your back.

In terms of combatting anxious thoughts, you can challenge these in your journal as well. You can do this informally, by taking a moment at the end of your daily journal to check for any assumptions, or negative thought patterns, you might have written about. If you identify any, try gently challenging them—ask yourself whether your assumption is always true, or if there are other options you could consider. You can do this more formally, using a column system. In the first, write down your issue, in the second, your feelings about it, and in the third, what you are thinking. Then in the fourth, go back and examine your thoughts, looking for evidence for and against them. In the final column, write down the realistic version of your thoughts, with what you've learnt. Using several of these techniques as and when you need to will help you manage and minimise your anxiety.

Mindfulness

Practicing mindfulness can be another beneficial way of regulating your emotions and any anxiety, and soothing your brain. Based on a form of meditation, it involves cultivating an awareness of your body, thoughts and surrounding environment in the present moment. Mindfulness is all about practicing acceptance, noting your thoughts and feelings and letting them pass across your mind without judgement. Try not to attach your attention to any one thought, negative or positive, but just let each float past you as it comes up. This helps you center yourself in the present and put your thoughts in perspective.

Mindfulness originated in Buddhism, but a secular version of it has become increasingly popular, as people have realised the incredible benefits it can bring. It is a powerful tool for regulating your emotions, increasing positivity and reducing negative emotions and stress. Getting in touch with your mind helps boost your sense of self, and can clarify your beliefs and what is important to you, making you more resilient, kind and confident. Practicing mindfulness is another way to mould our brains, helping the areas associated with empathy, memory, emotions and knowledge.

Mindfulness can also have an impact on our bodies—like journaling, engaging in a long term mindfulness practice can help our immune systems respond quicker to threats. The benefits of being calmer and less stressed are also reflected in the improved quality of sleep you might experience as a result of your practice. Making your journal practice more mindful is a great way to supercharge the results of journaling, and can be done very easily.

A lot of reflective journaling is naturally mindful, but there are some extra touches you can add to fully embrace mindful journaling. I have not discussed any preparation to do before you journal, because I did not want to make the process any more complicated or discouraging, but once you are settled in your journaling routine, incorporating a few quick exercises in before you start writing can be a really quick and easy way of making your journaling more mindful!

You can start by focusing on your breath, and trying to enter a state of mindfulness before you put pen to paper. This might be easier to do with a trigger, such as a short breath exercise. Take in a deep breath for seven seconds, hold it for four, and then breathe out for eight seconds. Repeating this exercise a few times will make you aware of your breathing, and soothe any anxieties you might be carrying in your chest. When you feel calm, return to a normal breathing pattern, and pick up your pen.

If this is not enough, you can try a more active exercise, like walking meditation. Pick a short distance that is clear of any obstacles, and walk up and down it. Try to focus on your movements—how does your body feel in movement? Which bits of your body are moving? How do your feet feel when they touch the ground, and when they return? This process is slightly different to going for a walk, another useful way of calming your mind and focusing your attention, because it is less about where you go or what you see, and more about tracking how your body moves and feels. Using this as a trigger for your journaling can be a valuable way of starting the conversation with yourself that you will continue in your journal.

You can continue this mindfulness journey into your writing, keeping a few simple guidelines in mind. The first one is that mindfulness is about engaging your whole body. So when you describe anything, make sure you are engaging all of your senses. It can be easy to focus on what we see and hear, but try to consider what you can smell, taste and feel as well. Thinking about your body as a coherent whole, instead of a few select parts, can help you feel more grounded, and reduce anxieties. In contrast, it can also be beneficial to focus on the little things. Pick a small detail from your day, and write in depth about it.

Slowing down and considering these details, like a beautiful flower you saw, or the sunshine reflecting on a windowpane, can be a really valuable way to take more care in your everyday existence, and ultimately lead a more mindful life.

Manifestations

Manifestations go hand in hand with the Goal Setting technique I discussed in Chapter Four, as they are all about looking towards the future, and making that future a reality. We might all be familiar with the concept of manifesting what we want, but without intention and purpose, often these are just empty phrases that have no concrete bearing on the direction of our lives. Using the Law of Attraction, we make sure our manifestations are directional and intentional, and therefore more likely to result in success.

The Law of Attraction is a simple maxim to keep in mind when journaling, that whatever you give your energy to, you will attract into your life. If you focus on negative things, you will attract more negativity, but if you focus on positive things, your life will become more positive. Therefore, you might want to use future facing manifestations alongside reflective Gratitude Journaling, in order to create a double pronged happiness strategy.

To create a manifestation, begin by writing a script. This is similar to journaling about your ideal life, except in a script you deliberately write as if you have already achieved all your goals. So instead of writing "I want to become a doctor," you might write "Today I start my first day as a paediatrician. I am so excited." Always using present tense. Make your script specific and believable—don't just put "I am rich beyond my wildest dreams," but focus in on what you have done to become rich, and what you can do with your money.

Explain why you want to achieve these goals as well, so in our doctor example we might go on to write "I have always wanted to work with children, helping them feel better, and I am so glad to have this sense of purpose and fulfilment in my career." This incorporates the motivations behind your dreams, and the gratitude you will feel when you achieve them. You can combine these scripts into a list of manifestations, which you can reread when you need motivation to continue working towards your goals.

CONCLUSION

Throughout these pages I have given you my knowledge and experience of journaling, and tried to impress upon you how much I believe it could change your life. Hopefully now you have some sense of why I believe this, and the range of benefits it can bring you.

Journaling is so powerful it can retrain your brain, taking advantage of your neuroplasticity to mould you into new patterns of thought. Putting in this work can help you control your emotions and get rid of negative thought patterns. This can help alleviate symptoms of trauma, anxiety and other mental health issues. In turn, it can also help you improve your mood, taking the time to feel gratitude for what you have, and working out how to attain what you have not. Giving you self-awareness is vital to helping you take control, and stop feeling like your life is running away from you.

As I have also mentioned, journaling can also have a physical impact on your wellbeing. If you feel disassociated from your body, which is more common than you might think given how much of our lives is now based in technology and online platforms, the act of writing a journal can help you root yourself back in your body, and gain a new sense of appreciation for it. This is also aided by the improvements journaling can make to your body, helping your immune system, your sleep patterns and your organs recover from the effects of stress.

Due to these benefits, there is an increasing field of research and information around journaling. While this can be incredibly valuable, it can also be disorientating and confusing to navigate the conflicting opinions around journaling. I hope that I have been able to cut through the noise, and pinpoint some key skills and techniques for you to take to heart. The first of these is the importance of making your journaling a daily habit, as without that structure, you will not be able to build up the self-awareness and discipline so essential to the journaling project. It is easy to say "Make this a habit," as many guides do, without acknowledging the difficulties of creating a habit. My career as a personal trainer has made me well aware of the difficulties of establishing a routine, especially when the task might initially seem arduous or overwhelming.

While the daily aspect of journaling makes your life a whole lot easier, it is not essential, just highly recommended. There are more benefits to be had with more regular inputs, but if you are still picking up a pen and writing with intention from time to time, this is certainly more meritable than nothing.

However, using the tips and tricks I have given you, you should now feel confident that you can work to create these healthy routines for you, learning more about yourself and how you work best in the process. To help you start the process, Chapter Four provides a foundational set of techniques—and you can use these as building blocks to form your journaling practice.

A daily schedule will form the backbone of your journal, but there are plenty of ways to do this, if a simple list does not work for you. Optimizing your schedule to be focused, pleasing and goal-orientated can quickly have an effect on the way that you work and live your life, and you will be surprised by how much more time you have, once you start using some of it to journal. Several of the techniques I have mentioned are useful to target specific issues in your life, or to combat specific emotions, and these you can swap in and out of your practice when necessary. These can also be used in conjunction with the training plans I outlined in Chapter Five, which can provide a useful starting point for your journaling if needed, or can be a useful addition to solve any problems you notice coming up in your regular practice.

These plans and techniques are designed to be as simple and as easy to use as possible, namely because I want you to be able to use them! I want you to be able to put down this book and immediately pick up a journal. This might sound demanding, but I firmly believe that once you know about the benefits of journaling, you will of course want to bring these into your life as soon as possible. Why would you delay starting a process that will bring you everything you want, and propel you towards your ideal life? Yes, it might be a long process, and there might be setbacks, but with your journal, you will be armed with the persistence to keep working, and the confidence to weather any storm life tries to throw at you. I believe journaling is best done with a purpose, and what higher purpose is there than to try to lead the best life possible, and transform yourself into the best version of yourself possible? Your journal is a guaranteed safe space for you to grow, support and push yourself into this new self, and I urge you to get started immediately.

REFERENCES

Ackerman, C. (2019, July 10). *83 Benefits of Journaling for Depression, Anxiety, and Stress.* Positive Psychology. https://positivepsychology.com/benefits-of-journaling/

Adams, K. (n.d.). *A Brief History of Journal Writing – The Center for Journal Therapy.* Center for Journal Therapy. https://journaltherapy.com/get-training/short-program-journal-to-the-self/journal-to-the-self/journal-writing-history/

Alvarez, K. (2016, January 26). *Thorough Guide to the Bullet Journal System.* Tiny Ray of Sunshine. https://www.tinyrayofsunshine.com/blog/bullet-journal-guide

Amy. (2016, March 21). *Journaling Techniques for Healing.* Stronginsideout.com. https://stronginsideout.com/journaling-techniques/

April 27, A. S. ·, & 2020. (2020, April 27). *25 Journal Prompts For Self-Love*. Self Love Circle. https://selflovecircle.co.uk/self-love-journal-prompts/

Axelrod, J. (2016, May 17). *The Health Benefits of Journaling*. Psych Central. https://psychcentral.com/lib/the-health-benefits-of-journaling#3

B, M. M. (2018, April 20). *A Guide To Writing Unsent Letters*. Just Write #JustPickUpANotepad. http://justpickupanotepad.blogspot.com/2018/04/a-guide-to-writing-unsent-letters.html

Babauta, L. (2007, June 21). *15 Ways to Create an Hour a Day of Extra Time ... for Solitude*. Zen Habits. https://zenhabits.net/15-ways-to-create-an-hour-a-day-of-extra-time-for-solitude/

badgesforall. (2020, January 8). T*he History of Journaling and Famous Journals*. Badges for All. https://badgesforall.org/2020/01/08/the-history-of-journaling-and-famous-journals/

Baikie, K. A., & Wilhelm, K. (2005). *Emotional and physical health benefits of expressive writing*. Advances in Psychiatric Treatment, 11(5), 338–346. https://doi.org/10.1192/apt.11.5.338

Bailey, K. (2018, July 31). *5 Powerful Health Benefits of Journaling*. Intermountain Healthcare. https://intermountainhealthcare.org/blogs/topics/live-well/2018/07/5-powerful-health-benefits-of-journaling/

Bartlett, J. (2019, July 3). *Depth-journaling, releasing the steam valve on repressed emotions*. Alight Intuition. https://www.alightintuition.com/personal-growth/depth-journaling-releasing-the-steam-valve-on-repressed-emotions/

Bastos, S. (2020, March 19). *7 Ways You Can Use Your Journal to Instantly Soothe Anxiety*. Medium. https://silviabastos.medium.com/7-ways-you-can-use-your-journal-to-instantly-soothe-anxiety-3e72b7d20958

Bokhari, D. (2017, May 2). *6 Journaling Ideas for Self-Development and Self-Discovery*. Dean Bokhari - Self Improvement Classes. https://www.deanbokhari.com/journaling-ideas/

Bulkeley, K. (2017, May 27). *Keeping a Dream Journal*. Psychology Today. https://www.psychologytoday.com/gb/blog/dreaming-in-the-digital-age/201705/keeping-dream-journal

Bullet Journal. (2018). *Learn*. Bullet Journal. https://bulletjournal.com/pages/learn

Chick, N. (2013, February 9). *Metacognition*. Vanderbilt University Center for Teaching. https://cft.vanderbilt.edu/guides-sub-pages/metacognition/

Evernote Team. (2015, August 3). *How Ryder Carroll Designed Bullet Journal*. Evernote Blog. https://evernote.com/blog/how-ryder-carroll-designed-bullet-journal/#:~:text=Ryder%20Carroll%2C%20a%20New%20York

Fagan, D. (n.d.). *Journal prompts & ideas for emotional release*. My TMS Journey. https://mytmsjourney.com/resources/journal-prompts-ideas-for-emotional-release/

Foroux, D. (2016, August 18). *How To Journal For Self-Improvement*. Darius Foroux. https://dariusforoux.com/how-to-journal/

FreelanceWriting. (2016, July 21). *A Powerful Journaling Tool - The Unsent Letter*. FreelanceWriting. https://www.freelancewriting.com/journal-writing/a-powerful-journaling-tool-the-unsent-letter/

Gillett, R. (2016, June 17). *Albert Einstein, Steve Jobs, and Benjamin Franklin Shared This Daily Habit*. Inc. https://www.inc.com/business-insider/steve-jobs-einstein-benjamin-franklin-daily-habit-improve-life.html

Goldberg, J. (2018, February 23). *Here Are The 50 Best Journaling Prompts You Will Ever Read Or Need*. Thought Catalog. https://thoughtcatalog.com/jeremy-goldberg/2018/02/here-are-the-50-best-journaling-prompts-you-will-ever-read-or-need/

Hage, J. (2020, September 1). *28 Confidence Journal Prompts to Improve Your Self-Esteem {Free Printable}*. Filling the Jars. https://www.fillingthejars.com/confidence-journal-prompts/

Harding, T. (2018, September 20). *32 Self-Love Journal Prompts*. TH. https://tiaharding.com/32-self-love-journal-prompts/

Hugo. (2021, January 14). *Journaling For Happiness: The Complete Guide*. Tracking Happiness. https://www.trackinghappiness.com/journaling-for-happiness/

Itani, O. (2020, January 29). *Solitude: The Importance and Benefits of Spending Time Alone.* Omar Itani. https://www.omaritani.com/blog/spending-time-alone

Ivana. (2019, August 18). *How to Use Positive Affirmations in Art Journaling and Change Your Mindset.* Artful Haven. https://artfulhaven.com/positive-affirmations-and-art-journaling/

Jestine. (2019, November 12). *Stream of Consciousness: A Different Take on Journaling.* Rediscover Analog. http://rediscoveranalog.com/stream-of-consciousness-a-different-take-on-journaling/

Kenyon, J. (2015, April 12). *12 highly influential people share the morning routines that set them up for success.* Business Insider. https://www.businessinsider.com/successful-people-share-morning-routines-2015-4?op=1/&r=US&IR=T#billionaire-john-paul-dejoria-starts-his-day-the-same-way-no-matter-where-he-is-4

Kira. (2018, January 6). *Mindful Journaling: 50 Unique Topics And Writing Tips For Beginners.* YBTT. https://www.yourbodythetemple.com/mindful-journalling/

Leyba, E. (2019, April 1). *Journaling Can Boost Happiness in Five Minutes or Less.* Psychology Today.

https://www.psychologytoday.com/gb/blog/joyful-parenting/201904/journaling-can-boost-happiness-in-five-minutes-or-less

Li, C. (2020, July 14). *How to start (and keep) a dream journal*. The Creative Independent. https://thecreativeindependent.com/guides/how-to-start-and-keep-a-dream-journal/

Litemind. (2007, November 6). *Tackle Any Issue With a List of 100*. Litemind. https://litemind.com/tackle-any-issue-with-a-list-of-100/

Madeson, M. (2020, June 14). *Self-Esteem Journals, Prompts, PDFs and Ideas*. PositivePsychology.com. https://positivepsychology.com/self-esteem-journal-prompts/

McCarthy, M. L. (n.d.). *Journaling Power: Build Self Confidence*. Create Write Now. https://www.createwritenow.com/journal-writing-blog/bid/101521/Journal-Power-Build-Self-Confidence

McKay, B., & McKay, K. (2014, May 12). *What Good Shall I Do This Day?* The Art of Manliness. https://www.artofmanliness.com/articles/what-good-shall-i-do-this-day/

Meier, T. (2016, February 1). *What Is a Journal - Journal Ideas and Inspiration.* Creative Writing Now. https://www.creative-writing-now.com/what-is-a-journal.html

Meyer, A. (2018, January 22). *Here's How to Actually Make Journaling a Habit.* Shine. https://advice.theshineapp.com/articles/heres-how-to-actually-make-journaling-a-habit/

Mindfulness Definition | What Is Mindfulness. (n.d.). Greater Good. https://greatergood.berkeley.edu/topic/mindfulness/definition#why-practice-mindfulness

Moldoveanu, M. C., & Martin, R. L. (2010). *Diaminds: Decoding the Mental Habits of Successful Thinkers.* University of Toronto Press. https://books.google.co.uk/books?id=G3wrwl4GjlsC&pg=PA70&lpg=PA70&dq=john+holland+three+covarying+variables&source=bl&ots=lMpLGFzPwE&sig=qZHedCDW_mLNb2HEUmUKeTQJ_tw&hl=en&sa=X&redir_esc=y#v=onepage&q=john%20holland%20three%20covarying%20variables&f=false

Naujalyte, B. (2018, June 18). *75 Journaling Prompts for Your Best Life.* The Bliss Bean. https://www.theblissbean.com/blog/2018/6/18/75-journaling-prompts-for-your-best-life

Nicole. (2021). *Bullet Journal Setup*. 101planners.com. https://www.101planners.com/wp-content/uploads/2017/01/How-to-setup-a-bullet-journal.jpg

Norton, M. (2016, February 15). *Journal for the Future*. Time Capsule Company. https://www.timecapsule.com/time-capsule/journal-for-the-future/

Pietrangelo, A. (2017, June 5). *The Effects of Stress on Your Body*. Healthline. https://www.healthline.com/health/stress/effects-on-body#Central-nervous-and-endocrine-systems

Pryle, M. (2019, November 20). *Never-Fail 5-Step Character Sketch Writing Activity*. Middle Web. https://www.middleweb.com/41629/five-step-never-fail-character-sketching/

Purcell, M. (2016, May 17). *The Health Benefits of Journaling*. Psych Central. https://psychcentral.com/lib/the-health-benefits-of-journaling#1

Reat, L. C., PhD, ATR. (2019, May 21). *Journaling for Inner Guidance: the Wisdom of Your Other Hand*. Medium. https://medium.com/@luciaccapa/journaling-for-inner-guidance-the-wisdom-of-your-other-hand-c18e8394ea16

Roberts, E. (2019). *23 Journal Prompts to Improve Your Self-Esteem*. Healthy Place. https://www.healthyplace.com/blogs/buildingselfesteem/2015/07/journal-to-improve-self-esteem

Ryan, E. (2014, November 28). *Top 10 Historically Important Notebooks*. TopTenz. https://www.toptenz.net/top-10-historically-important-notebooks.php

Scott, E. (2019a). *Here Are Ways You Can Journal Your Way out of Anxiety*. Verywell Mind. https://www.verywellmind.com/journaling-a-great-tool-for-coping-with-anxiety-3144672

Scott, E. (2019b). *Is Journaling an Effective Stress Management Tool?* Verywell Mind. https://www.verywellmind.com/the-benefits-of-journaling-for-stress-management-3144611

Scott, S. J. (n.d.). *10 Tips for Mindful Writing and Meditative Journaling*. Develop Good Habits. https://www.developgoodhabits.com/mindful_writing/

Scott, S. J. (2016, January 19). *How to Form a New Habit (in 8 Easy Steps)*. Develop Good Habits.

https://www.developgoodhabits.com/how-to-form-a-habit-in-8-easy-steps/

Scriveiner. (2019, October 29). *History of Journaling.* https://www.scriveiner.com/post/history-of-journaling

Sicinski, A. (2009, March 7). *The Complete Guide on How to Mind Map for Beginners.* IQ Matrix Blog. https://blog.iqmatrix.com/how-to-mind-map

Simmons, M. (n.d.). *I spent years discovering the simple tactics gurus like Oprah, Einstein, and Buffett used to become successful—here they are.* Quartz. https://qz.com/1054094/i-spent-years-discovering-the-simple-tactics-gurus-like-oprah-einstein-and-buffett-used-to-become-successful-here-they-are/

Smyth, J. M., Johnson, J. A., Auer, B. J., Lehman, E., Talamo, G., & Sciamanna, C. N. (2018). *Online Positive Affect Journaling in the Improvement of Mental Distress and Well-Being in General Medical Patients With Elevated Anxiety Symptoms: A Preliminary Randomized Controlled Trial.* JMIR Mental Health, 5(4), e11290. https://doi.org/10.2196/11290

Smyth, J. M., Stone, A. A., Hurewitz, A., & Kaell, A. (1999). *Effects of Writing About Stressful Experiences on Symptom Reduction in Patients With Asthma or*

Rheumatoid Arthritis. JAMA, 281(14), 1304. https://doi.org/10.1001/jama.281.14.1304

Studio, M. (2018, July 23). *5 Celebrities Who Keep a Journal*. Medium. https://medium.com/@mintestudio/5-celebrities-who-keep-a-journal-a6888bc2a42b

Swenson, M. (2018, March 26). *The Astonishing History of Journaling*. Epica. https://epica.com/blogs/epica-news/the-astonishing-history-of-journaling

Syring, E. (2019, September 26). *How to Use Journaling to Manifest With the Law of Attraction.* Create Your Best Life. https://sheslivingherbestlife.com/how-to-manifest-journaling/

Tartakovsky, M. (2012, May 2). *4 Journaling Exercises to Help You Manage Your Emotions*. Psych Central. https://psychcentral.com/blog/4-journaling-exercises-to-help-you-manage-your-emotions#4

The Art of Journaling: *How To Start Journaling, Benefits of Journaling, and More*. (2020, January 31). Daily Stoic. https://dailystoic.com/journaling/#heading4

The Positive Author. (2020, December 18). *5 Prompts To Create Positive Affirmations For Morning Journaling*. The Positive Author.

http://www.thepositiveauthor.com/5-prompts-to-create-positive-affirmations-for-morning-journaling/

thejoywithin. (2019, June 11). *How to Keep a Daily Affirmation Journal*. Thejoywithin. https://thejoywithin.org/empowerment-exercises/how-to-keep-a-daily-affirmation-journal-ideas-prompts-and-examples

Theresa. (2021). *The Journal in Trauma Therapy*. Dis-Sos.com. https://www.dis-sos.com/journal-in-trauma-therapy/

Thompson, K. (2017, May 17). *7 Tips to Organize Your Life With a Simple Notebook*. How Does She. https://howdoesshe.com/organize-your-life-with-notebook/

Tull, M. (2020, December 14). *How to Use Journaling to Cope With PTSD*. Verywell Mind. https://www.verywellmind.com/how-to-use-journaling-to-cope-with-ptsd-2797594

Uimari, K. (2017, December 20). *7 Mental Health Journal Prompts for Stress Relief*. Rose-Minded. https://www.rose-minded.com/post/mental-health-journal-prompts-for-stress-relief

Unsplash. (2017, September 30). *Photo by Estée Janssens on Unsplash*. Unsplash.com. https://unsplash.com/photos/mO3s5xdo68Y

Vardy, M. (2018, March 6). *Why You Shouldn't Spend Time Journaling In The Morning (And What You Should Do Instead)*. Productivityist. https://productivityist.com/no-morning-journaling/

Ye, B. (2019, February 17). *How To Journal In The Morning (And Why)*. Medium. https://writingcooperative.com/how-to-journal-in-the-morning-and-why-274ed0a2bb63

Young, S. H. (2007, August 14). *18 Tricks to Make New Habits Stick*. Lifehack; Lifehack. https://www.lifehack.org/articles/featured/18-tricks-to-make-new-habits-stick.html

Printed in Great Britain
by Amazon